SO-AXN-178

MEAN TIME LOVE:

SO I'VE GOT SELF-LOVE, NOW WHAT?

Anita Ross

Copyright © 2018 by Anita Ross

All rights reserved, including the right of reproduction in whole or in part in any form without the prior written permission of the publisher.

Published in the United States by: Anita Ross

Printed in the United States of America

For information about special discounts on bulk purchases, please send inquiries to: info@anitaross.net

Front cover design by: Juan Millan & Patricia E. Aguas Millan

Back cover design & layout by: Jesse Bloodworth

Photos by: Rhonda Gutierrez

Edited by: Maria Pelaez

Library of Congress Control Number: 2018901506

ISBN: 978-0-692-05414-7

1ˢᵗ Edition, March 2018

It is Anita Ross' mission to empower millions of women to love themselves fully and to equip them with the tools to do so. To find out more about booking Anita for speaking engagements or workshops, please visit us at: www.anitaross.net

This book is dedicated to my exquisite, extraordinary, powerful and inspiring children Angelina, Kameela and Khaiden. You remind mommy everyday what love is, what it looks like and what it feels like. Your love fuels my commitment to creating a world that honors your magnificence.

FOREWORD

In the first several years of my recovery from drug addiction, I was told all the time how I needed to just 'love myself.' I would say, "Yeah-yeah, I do love myself. I get up every day, go to work, brush my teeth, wear decent clothes and I'm in recovery. So that must be self-love, right?"

Little did I know that while I had some success in recovering from crack cocaine, that the reconstruction and rediscovery of my authentic self was going to take more than I could possibly imagine, and that I had a long road ahead of me.

You see, I had no idea that self-love was based on loving my authentic self – the very essence of who I was created to be. I had no idea how much the insidious nature of low self-esteem, self-judgment, self-loathing, and the belief that I wasn't good enough was operating in every area of my life. Quite frankly, I just thought that life sucked – and that my fortune or misfortune was based on people, places and outer circumstances.

I was operating under the misguided notion that someone or something outside of myself had taken my power away. But I have come to understand that no one has the authority to take my power away. I never lost my power – I had simply disconnected from it. Your power, mastery, authority and dominion is ***who you are*** and no one has the power to take it away! You may have inadvertently disconnected from it, but you have never lost it.

In this amazing book, Anita Ross states that now is the time, more than ever to wake up where we have fallen asleep and numbed out to our own power. Her description of self-worth drives us deeper into the true meaning of self-love. It is not just about the basic necessities of self-care – anyone can do that. It is about remembering your authentic self – and standing in the "Self" that you were created to be – no matter what. When we return to that level of self-awareness, self worth is revealed, and self-love is the result – and nothing can shake us from that conviction.

Anita Ross, is a woman who has found the blessing in the many bottoms she has experienced prior to reconnecting to her authentic self. She has transformed her test into a testimony, and her mess into a message of hope, inspiration, and kick-butt motivation to those of us who have disconnected from our true identities of powerful, amazing and brilliant beings.

You are being supported in this book to reconnect to your true identity of worthiness, of being "more than enough" and your *greatness* - because that's who you really are – no matter how many curve balls life has thrown at you.

As we honor our experiences, vulnerability and humanity, we are going to falter, waiver, waffle, and even fall, but when we make a decision to return to our authentic selves no matter what – we get back up again – stronger, clearer, more loving, open, and fiercer than ever!

Anita Ross is "fierce," tenacious, brilliant, kind, generous, and clear about who she is and what she was created to be. She is here to remind you of that same truth about yourself, and she does so in her new book *Mean Time Love: So I've Got Self-Love, Now What?* with the conviction and authority of one who has fallen, faltered, forgotten, and has gotten back up with a testimony and message to share that will change your life – if you listen!

I am so honored to write this foreword for my sister-girl and colleague. She is the real deal, and I am blessed to know her.

Ester Nicholson,
Author of *Soul Recovery*,
Speaker, Recovery Specialist

CONTENTS

PREFACE

I teach from a very honest place. I don't know any other way. In fact, many people have wondered how I do it. How do I speak so openly about being sexually assaulted or about my multiple stints in physically and emotionally abusive relationships? Or the downward spiral of poor choices that resulted from a dwindling self-esteem as each blow took its toll and ultimately landed me in a rock-bottom, life-changing moment. The short answer is that I'm healed from it all. I no longer have an emotional attachment to the pain I once experienced. As a result, I can get through telling my story without bursting into tears, having any other noticeable reaction or internalizing any negative feelings. It wasn't until I reached this point of healing that I started sharing the lessons I've learned about achieving unconditional self-love and total self-acceptance.

Also, I had built my "self-love muscle" to the point of withstanding any level of feedback and had gotten crystal clear on my purpose. You see, operating at this level of vulnerability requires us to love ourselves even if our message is not received in a positive way and to stay the course when we're on a mission! We don't get to redirect, go off on a tangent or close up shop, because someone doesn't like what we've got to say. As long as the context of our message is love, those who are meant to receive it will receive it. I have always maintained this as the truth and am so grateful that so many amazing women have been positively impacted by this *Mean Time Love* movement that has come to life since I chose to share myself in an unprecedented way - - a way that I had never done prior to my healing.

I am going to tell you a secret. The woman I wrote about in my first book, is not the woman I write about in this one! I am so far removed from the woman who experienced herself as broken. I can see her, speak about her, learn from her and I still love her, but I am no longer her. Don't get me wrong my "old self" tries to sneak up on me and take over my thoughts, behaviors and actions at times, but that is what this book is all about: How to maintain our position, footing, and submersion in self-love when the going gets rough.

With that said, sharing this book with the world feels more vulnerable than the first go round. In this book, I share who I am now. Perfect in my imperfections. Strong in my weaknesses. Courageous in my fears. Growing in my moments of unwillingness to do so. All of it culminating in an authentic, vulnerable and purpose-driven message from me to you. And I say, you're worth it.

Disclosure: Please be advised that in order to protect the identity of any persons mentioned in this book, actual names and details have not been used where appropriate.

ACKNOWLEDGMENTS

I thank my husband Kevin for loving me unconditionally and teaming up with me in this twisty, bendy, bumpy thing called life. You're fun, gorgeous and inspiring. You hold me to my highest even when I don't feel like stretching to get there and yet you see me through to the finish line every time. You're a total package and I couldn't have dreamed up a better partner. I choose you. Thank you for choosing me.

I thank my mother and father for loving me with everything you've got. I am convinced I came through the darkness to find my light because of the deep love you instilled in me.

I thank my sister, Lisa, for co-creating a fun, loving and meaningful sisterhood. It continues to amaze me how we are there for each other like no other can be. My love and appreciation for the woman you are, grows each day. Plus, you are the best Tia ever!!!

I thank Aixa, Tina, Gabriel, Chakshu, Michael, Roberto, Margo and Rohan for being the "A-Team" of cousins! I know we are far apart but the love I have for you transcends distance and I hope you can feel it. You are all absolutely exquisite.

I thank my Uncle Roque, Aunt Robin, Aunt Donna, Uncle Ray, Aunt Norma and Uncle David for making me feel like the most loved niece in the world! I feel your support today as strongly as I did when I was a little girl. How precious is that? I hope you know how much I love and appreciate each of you. And thank you for always being so wonderful to my children. They love you so much too!

I thank my Grandpa Seymour for loving me and my family the way you do. I am truly grateful for your love, wisdom and humorous take on life. It brings me such joy.

I thank Maria Pelaez for taking the concept of BFF to a whole new level of joy and fulfillment. You see me through the ups and downs of life with such ease and grace. Nothing ever seems too big, or too small, for you to give me your undivided love and attention. I am beyond grateful for you and I love you so much! Your dedication, talent and beautiful heart played a significant role in making this the best book it could be. Thank you for stepping up once again as Editor, knowing the commitment it takes. We did it again!

I thank Misty for being my "dih-dern" *[how my daughter said the word 'sister' while she was mastering the art of talking and it stuck with us]*. No matter how near or far, your wisdom, humor and support are always on point and perfectly timed. Our bond is strong and always will be. I love you beyond measure.

I thank Ceonita for being a constant reminder of what it looks like to stay true to who you are and always reeling me in with the "Ceo side of things" when I'm out there on a limb. Thank you for loving me and my babies the way you do. You make Sacramento feel like "home." Okay that's enough, you have a whole dang chapter.

I thank Freda "Mimi" Shadlow for always looking beyond all the roles I play in life, to truly see the woman that I am. I treasure you're gentle but steadfast approach to loving me and 'our' babies. Thank you for the tireless hours spent taking care of them so I could take the Mean Time Love message out to the world.

I thank Margie McCutcheon for taking such great care of me on so many of my "Mommy Daycations" that were used to write this book. You fed my tummy well but my soul even better. I love you.

I thank Ester Nicholson for being the best sister-friend a girl could ask for! Our love is strong like it's stood the test of a lifetime and I'm so enjoying every minute of it!

I thank my Spiritual Mother, the Reverend Dr. Georgia Prescott, for accepting me into your life, your spiritual community and into Sacramento with open arms, no questions asked. I love you.

I thank Sylvia High for being a pillar of strength, wisdom and guidance for me and the world. I'm so grateful for your mentorship.

I thank Candy, David, Megan, April, Kristee, Tehya and Kendall for being my "family" away from home. May you always know how much I value each of you and the role you play in my life. I love you all so much.

I thank Ahlonis, Nia, Veronica, Sandra, Crystal as well as all other Mean Time Love graduates, readers and students of the work, for trusting me with a little piece of your journey to acknowledging your magnificence and owning your power. It's truly an honor.

I thank Unity of Sacramento for consistently being a community I can simply be myself in and always feel enfolded in pure unconditional love. You are truly a force for good in the world!

INTRODUCTION

Now more than ever, I am aware of the urgent need for women to learn the significance and power of self-love. Women are being discriminated against. Women are being disempowered. Women are being sexually assaulted. Women are being belittled. Women are being sexually objectified. Women are underrepresented and underpaid. Women are tearing down other women [as a result of their own self-loathe]. It is time for change!

Self-love is not only the healing agent for these ills but it is also the key to our awakening. We must wake up to our worth! It's more than just knowing how to arrive at self-love, it's knowing how to stay there. It's easier for us to stay the course of self-love when things are going well. But let's face it, life also offers us mind-boggling, nerve-racking, stomach-turning, pain-inducing, trauma-causing experiences that try to shake us to our core and they will win if you aren't fully steeped in the *process* of self-love: *To **know**, to **love** and to **express** your authentic self.*

Knowing yourself entails:
- ❦ Being conscious of your inherent worth
- ❦ Having a clear understanding of your morals, values and spirituality
- ❦ Checking in with how you have transformed, on an ongoing basis

Loving yourself entails:
- ❦ Accepting and appreciating yourself just as you are, no matter what your circumstances are, what you have

experienced in the past or what other people think of you

❧ Extending kindness, forgiveness and generosity to yourself

❧ Championing and affirming yourself

Expressing yourself entails:

❧ Having the courage and confidence to be authentic in all areas of your life

❧ Aligning your behaviors and actions with who you know yourself to be

❧ Having honest communication with yourself and others

❧ Making choices that align with your inherent worth - - your greatest good

All of this, all of the time! Self-love is an ongoing process. These three aspects of self-love are interdependent and are equally important. You can't have one without the others and still achieve self-love. You will find that self-love calls on you to continually recommit to knowing, loving and expressing yourself. At times it can be a tall order, but the reward is extraordinary living. *The life of your dreams is a string of extraordinary moments produced by you, and for you, that results from the process of self-love.*

With that said, if we are not mindful of the ongoing nature of self-love, we run the risk of being triggered into inauthentic thoughts, beliefs, choices, actions and/or bhaviors. Anytime you operate inauthentically there will be pain, suffering and/or discomfort because you are out of alignment with the life you want to live. You will find yourself in a set of situations or circumstances, or around people that contrast your inherent worth, such as unhealthy relationships, unfulfilling careers, addiction, unhealthy weight gain or loss. None of which serve your highest good.

Triggers are those experiences that manage to take us there. Some typical triggers are:

- Fear
- People's thoughts, behaviors and/or actions towards you
- Loss of a loved one
    - Whether it be through death, the end of a relationship, divorce/breakup, abandonment, among others
- Adverse changes in financial status
- Diagnoses or medical conditions
- Aging and body changes
- Injustices - Racism, oppression, inequality, misogyny, etc.
- Unresolved childhood trauma
- Any other types of trauma not already mentioned above

I wrote this book as a sequel to *Mean Time Love: A Woman's Journey From Self-Loathe to Self-Love.* In that book I explored how to achieve your *mean* - - that place where you **unwaveringly** know, love and express yourself, no matter what! In this book, my intention is to support all women in **sustaining** self-love no matter what challenges come our way. Sure, there will be times when we have to process our emotions and heal from our pain, but there is a deep-rooted assurance that we will get back to our mean. It is in this way that we will own our power, stand up for our rights and make choices aligned with our dreams. When we hit critical mass of women operating from this place, there's no limit to what we can accomplish! You see when we love ourselves fully, the overflow of love has no where else to go but into our families, our communities and, ultimately, into the world. With this kind of love emanating from us, together, we can rid this world of all the ills that plague it. This is the vision that keeps me driven. It's the hope that keeps me inspired and it's the result

I wish to leave for my children: *A world that works for everyone!*

I realize the complexity and depth of the message I bring with me into this world - - **self-love** - - requires a whole lot of research and with that, comes proving firsthand that it works! Since stepping into my purpose, my primary assignment has been to share the distinctions of self-love that I've learned through my life experiences. However, I can't pretend that it's always been easy.

Amidst all the goodness of my life, there are days I feel like I'm wearing a mask and my truth is buried. There are instances when I avoid the pain at all costs, because I believe it may actually break me. There are times when someone asks me how I'm doing and I push out a meager "great," but in truth, everything within me just wants to scream "My life is in shambles!" Sometimes it's like I'm clinging to my *mean* for dear life. But from the breakdowns to the blessings, to the bad news and the good news, each day, I wake up in gratitude knowing that within all of it, there is a lesson for me. I am grateful to have tools in my back pocket that help me process and heal when necessary. I am thankful for knowing when to seek support and for a top notch support team.

In this gratitude, I ask you my dear friend, to come from behind your mask. Today is your day! Don't be afraid of the pain, embrace it because it is your path to freedom! Allow this book to guide you, back to you.

Please know that I am on your support team and I've got your back.

I love you.

A NOTE ABOUT THIS BOOK

Mean Time Love: So I've Got Self-Love, Now What? is comprised of distinctions, principles and perspectives that will open up your consciousness and make you available to transformation. To support you through your transformation, you are provided with tools and practical exercises that will empower you to know, love and express yourself as you traverse the hills and valleys of life.

Each chapter takes you on a journey through the following three phases:

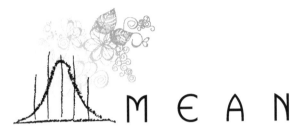 MEAN

Your *mean* is the place where you unceasingly know, love and express your authentic self regardless of your circumstances, your past or how others perceive you. In this section, you will read about some of the real life experiences that have challenged me to live from my mean even when it was painful, uncomfortable and/or scary.

 TIME

Time is the gift of patience you give yourself to reflect, interpret and learn from your experiences. In this section, I share the insights I gained from reflecting on my life and experiences.

 LOVE

Love is the gift I give to you. I close each chapter by sharing the knowledge, tools and wisdom that I used to navigate my life from my mean.

MESSAGE TO MY BELOVED READERS

On Motherhood...

In chapters Six and Nine, I talk about some of my challenges, victories, and insights as a mother. I understand motherhood is a complex, and at times painful, topic due to the societal expectation that women are to be mothers yet some of us have lost children, cannot have children or have chosen not to have children. Also, some of us have trauma in our relationship with our mothers. If you are sensitive for any of these reasons or any not mentioned, please take precaution, choose wisely when reading and be gentle with yourself. If you are open to exploring this pain, I can assure you, there is a healing available to you if you're willing to take the journey.

On Spirituality...

Spirituality is a holistic approach to the way you are connected with nature, the universe, God or however you identify a higher power in your life. We are all on our own, unique, spiritual paths and I honor all of them! For purposes of continuity and flow of this book, wherever I aim to present the idea of a greater guardian spirit outside of ourselves, I will reference "God" because it is the higher power of my understanding. Feel free to insert the higher power of your understanding as you read along.

Chapter 1

Get Your Fear In Check!

*"Because you never know where life is gonna take you
and you can't change where you've been.
But today, I have the opportunity to choose.
I used to have guilt about why things happen the way they
did because life is gone do what it do.
And everyday, I have the opportunity to choose...
And I choose to be the best that I can be.
I choose to be courageous in everything I do.
My past don't dictate who I am. I choose."*
- I Choose, A song by India Arie

 M E A N

I was so exhausted that my legs were on the brink of giving out. My back was providing lackluster support. I could barely process my thoughts or execute a sentence that made sense but I still had a long night ahead of me. I had just worked fourteen, twelve-hour days straight and was fed up with this kind of work schedule. While I was happy that I had an interview the next morning in a new state and in a totally new industry, the thought of getting on a flight at this point was draining. On top of that, my flight was not scheduled to arrive until just after midnight which made me a little nervous given that I didn't know much about where I was headed. My main concern was getting in and out of there so I could get back to work without my absence being noticed. We were in the middle of a new car launch and all engineers were expected to be on the premises during production in the event that something went wrong with our designs. As a young woman in the auto industry, there were some people waiting for me to "mess up" and I wanted to keep them all quiet.

I slept from the moment the flight attendant started announcing the safety procedures through the final descent. It was probably the best sleep I had in months. When I arrived, I waited what seemed like forever for my luggage and then headed to catch the hotel shuttle. When I got on the shuttle I verified the hotel address with the driver. He assured me that was where we were headed.

When I entered the lobby, I felt an eerie energy but I ignored it and went straight to the front desk. After searching for my reservation and the attendant eventually let me know that I was, in fact, at the wrong hotel. She called the shuttle for a return pick up and asked me to wait in the lobby.

At this point, I was afraid. I could not pinpoint why but I just felt extremely unsafe. I quickly called my boyfriend, with hopes that he could calm me down. I was increasingly getting frantic with each minute that passed and he kept asking me what was wrong. It was kind of bizarre but I was even looking around for a place to hide. My boyfriend says "get inside the lobby" and I just about yelled at him "I am in the lobby!" The minute those words came out of my mouth, two men entered the lobby with handguns and I just began to scream. The front desk attendant immediately ducked behind the counter while one of the men pointed the gun in my face. I could not compose myself. I was no longer able to think logically. My boyfriend was on the line completely confused and afraid of what may be happening to the woman he loved. As I trembled with fear and watched the barrel of the gun wave ever so slightly in front of my eyes, the man ripped my handbag and satchel from my shoulder and told me to "Shut the fuck up!" I tried but I just could not stop screaming. Simultaneously, the second armed man grabbed the other shuttle rider's laptop and handbag. Before they left the premises, the man who took my belongings gave me a strange look, kind of squinted his eyes at me, removed the weapon from my face and left the building.

It all happened in a matter of seconds and I was dazed in the aftermath. I was in shock but I knew it was time for me to compose myself. I watched as the front desk attendant came out from hiding and then I heard my boyfriend on the line calling my name. I put the phone to my ear and explained what had just happened. He asked if the police had been called and I didn't know the answer. Just as he suggests that I call the police, the low battery signal beeps on my cell phone. My ability to connect with anyone who could help, was running out with each beep so I got off the phone to preserve the battery. I knew I had an uncle who lived somewhere nearby, so I looked up his number. In that moment, the police walked through the door so I quickly jotted his number down in the event my phone died.

When the police asked for my statement, I told them my experience and gave them a vivid description of the perpetrators. I asked if they were going to search the neighborhood and they quickly said "No." The policeman proceeded to tell me that the thieves were long gone and my belongings had probably been discarded somewhere on the side of a road stripped of any valuables. He goes on to say that the criminals will immediately use my credit cards and if they have any identification documents, will try to open accounts under my name. As they said that I reached down in my pocket and felt my driver's license. Thank God it wasn't in my wallet, I had put it in my pocket after showing it to airport security.

After talking with the not-so-helpful cops, I called my great uncle and asked him to come get me. I felt bad waking him and my aunt up at this crazy hour but without hesitation, they came to get me.

It was approaching 3:00am by the time we got to their home and all I could think about was canceling my credit cards and booking an earlier flight back home. Before I knew it, it was 8:00am and it was time for me to notify my interviewer of what happened.

As I was explaining the incident to him and that I did not have any appropriate clothing or my required presentation, he asked me "Will you come in for the interview anyway?" I hesitated because the last thing I wanted to do was head in the direction of where I was mugged at gunpoint. I was also a bit taken aback that he would even ask me to do this under such awful circumstances. But then I realized that he simply wanted to meet with me because I was a good candidate for his team, so I agreed to come in.

Running on no sleep, wearing jeans with a tank top covered by my great aunt's 25-year-old blouse, flip-flops and cracked nail polish, I was certainly not feeling my best. But I was committed to giving it my best effort.

As I walked into the beautiful office building, I was getting some unpleasant stares and when I let the receptionist know I was here for an interview she looked at me like I was an intruder. When she called my potential new manager, I could hear her whispering to him about my appearance. I could tell he just let her know that he'd be right there.

I was in a small room with two interviewers shooting engineering and project management questions at me one after another. They were friendly and funny but also really efficient. They weren't wasting any time!

As I answered a barrage of questions, some of which I found to be difficult, I could literally feel God's strength and wisdom flow out of me with each response. I was rocking the interview! Before I left, both of them acknowledged me for having the courage and strength to show up. They were really impressed by that alone and my performance at the interview was icing on the cake.

I flew home right after the interview and had a hard time falling asleep because I kept replaying the previous night in my mind. Despite that, the next day I woke up clear about where I was headed. Even though many of my friends and family thought I was crazy, I accepted the job.

Can you believe it? This experience brings the total number of times I've been held at gunpoint up to three! If you've read *Mean Time Love: A Woman's Journey From Self-Loathe to Self-Love*, you know the other two times were at the hands of a boyfriend. I tell that story often when I'm teaching because it was a pivotal point in my life. It was my rockbottom moment and the start of my self-love journey. Perhaps that's why it upstages this experience [in my mind] but when I tell people I've been mugged at gunpoint, I instantly see the horror on their faces. They are even more shocked when I tell them that I moved to the very place where it happened. It is only then that I am reminded of how awful this experience was and how scary it can be for a person to hear or imagine.

I am not sure why I have always downplayed the scariness or difficulty of this event especially when there were quite a few obstacles resulting from it. I had a lot of bad dreams and sleepless nights. For over a year, my time and energy was expended on defending my identity to creditors, the Department of Motor Vehicles and retailers. This was so demoralizing because the burden of proof fell on my shoulders rather than on the criminals.

I also remember contacting the hotel manager to see if they would accept some responsibility for the incorrect shuttle routing and the lack of security on the premises. But when I finally got a response, the owner said "This happens everyday in this neighborhood and you're lucky you're alive." I found that to be an inhumane and absurd response. I was not satisfied so I decided to contact a lawyer. She was immediately interested in the case. This made me feel hopeful that I might get some justice but when she did her preliminary research she learned that the very same hotel line had already won several similar cases. She chose not to take the case and I was disappointed yet again.

Years later I realized I had some healing to do as a result of accepting the injustice and mistreatment regarding this experience. From the cop's unwillingness to search for my items as if I wasn't worth the effort. To the hardship of defending my identity while criminals were stealing in my name. To the hotel owner's flippant dismissal of the trauma I experienced. You see, no one has the right to disrespect, dishonor or dismiss us! We get to live with *dignity* no matter how inconvenient it is for others. *Dignity is our innate state of being worthy, honored or esteemed and our innate right to being respected.* It's true, people will not always be loving. Most of the time, it is because they are hurting. *Hurt people, hurt people.* As such, their behaviors, judgments and actions are a reflection of their own consciousness and growth. The key is that we don't let their choice to show up in the world this way, distract us from honoring our innate worth. We get to love ourselves enough to ensure we aren't left feeling victimized, unworthy or any other ways that don't serve us.

L O V E

Fear is here to stay. Doesn't that stink, especially since it is a major trigger for people? But it's true and we perpetuate it. Even though fear is not tangible it has a very powerful presence in our society. We are socialized with fear from our toddler years. Do you recall being told something like "Danger, danger! Don't touch!" anytime you went near an outlet? Or saying something like that when your child is headed for something that could hurt them? We can keep fear alive even when our intentions are good.

Let's face it, there are some scary things in this world and we do have to take precautions when necessary. The problem arises when fear paralyzes us or alters our willingness to be authentic. When we are too afraid to go for what we want because we believe the consequences will harm us in some way like failure, loss or pain. Here is what I offer as a win-win scenario: *Have your relationship with fear! If you want to entertain it, coddle it or even cozy up with it; that is fine! However, when it is time to take authentic action - - action that is aligned with your authentic self - - put that fear in check! Be brave and follow through with your courageous action to completion.* If compelled to, once you have manifested your true desire, go ahead and jump right back into bed with fear. Repeat this scenario in it's entirety, as needed. Just don't let fear stop you from living the life of your dreams!

Now let's take a look at the choice I made to move in spite of this terrifying event in my life. You see, even in the throes of tremendous adversity, your authentic self will shine through. *Your authentic voice is an underlying knowing, or awareness, of the direction to take when an opportunity to choose, presents itself.* In times of adversity, it is usually more comfortable to ignore this awareness, because most of the time, your authentic voice is calling forth courage. The courage to "go for it anyway"! You see, I could have scared myself into staying right where I was and convinced myself I was better off. At least I had a great pay-ing job. So what if I was essentially a workhorse. At least I had a boyfriend. So what if we were in completely different stages of our lives nor moving in a positive direction. At least I knew what to expect each day. So what if my life was on automatic and my heart wasn't in it. Well, my authentic voice had other plans. I was being called to let go of my safety net and head across the country in pursuit of my higher good.

It ended up being an amazing choice! I moved on to meet my husband and to actualize my purpose. Making these kind of bold moves require you to *be open, receptive and rejoice in affirmation from nature, the universe or a higher power, that you are taking authentic action.* I know God is with me at all times and in all ways but sometimes God puts a signature on it, just so we can be clear, beyond the shadow of a doubt, that there is a greater force working on our behalf. Here are some of those "signatures" that gave me confidence in my choice to take the new job:

- ❧ I came out of this extremely dangerous situation without physical harm even though I was screaming at the top of my lungs, practically inviting the armed robber to 'shut me up.'

- ❧ The perpetrators took everything I had except my phone and my driver's license allowing me to call for help and fly back home without any issues.

- ❧ I successfully answered complex engineering questions that I had never heard before while running on zero hours of sleep.

Together, these events built my confidence in the choice to comply with my authentic voice.

The last distinction I draw from this experience is the power of showing up. Have you ever had someone simply show up for you, they didn't have to say a word, and you felt their enormous love and support? I remember when I had my first book launch event and two of my friends surprised me by flying in from across the country to be there. I was busy signing books when I saw them through the corner of my eye and within seconds I was in tears. We hadn't even spoken yet and I could not contain myself. Their showing up demonstrated how much they love me and support the work that I do. It also said a heck of lot about their character. Both of them, Maxine and Kathy, have important jobs, lots of people depending on them and families to tend to, yet they took time out of their busy lives to let me know I matter to them. Showing up speaks volumes about who you are.

Along those same lines, that is what showing up to my interview did. It demonstrated courage, determination, commitment and teamwork. All that was left for them to ask about was my technical ability.

May this guide you the next time you question whether you are going to show up for a loved one, an opportunity or the world.

Chapter 2

Finding Peace In Your Pain

"Don't lose who you are, in the blur of the stars
Seeing is deceiving, dreaming is believing
It's okay not to be okay
Sometimes it's hard, to follow your heart
But tears don't mean you're losing, everybody's bruising...
There's nothing wrong with who you are"
- Who You Are, A song by Jessie J.

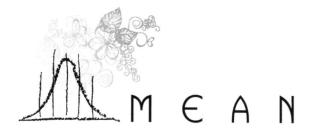 M E A N

It had been a typical morning. I dropped my girls off at their respective schools. I lifted weights at the gym while my son played in the kids club. I completed all my random errands. Then I went home to feed my baby his lunch and put him down for his nap. That was when things went off the beaten path.

I received a phone call from my husband. First thing he says is "Are you alone? Are you sitting down?" I'd heard this before, and it was never good, so I rushed him by saying, "Yes, yes, what's going on?" He proceeds to tell me that my seventy-year-old father had been attacked while walking through a snowstorm in Brooklyn, New York. Just around the corner from the home I grew up in, two men got my father into a chokehold and kicked him in the face until he fell to the ground. After taking his cash and wallet, they left him in the snow. Soon after it occurred, a woman found him laying half way underneath a car. With his guidance, she was able to help him get home. When they rang the bell, my mom answered the door…to her horror. Between the blood and the swelling, she could hardly recognize him. My dad was then taken to the Emergency Room.

I could not believe what I was hearing. Sharp pains were shooting through my heart and I felt like I was in shock. Knowing that my father was essentially left for dead in a snowstorm and there was nothing I could do about it, was killing me. My husband let me know that I was incoherent at this point so I chose to get off the phone. I grabbed the blanket on my bed so hard that my knuckles were white. I put the blanket over my mouth so my screaming wouldn't wake up my baby. My heart was breaking and I couldn't control the extreme emotions. One minute I was crying and the next, I was so angry that I wanted to bash the walls in.

Hours later, I was exhausted but I heard my son calling for me, so I went to get him. I picked him up from his crib and hugged him so tight. He gave me just the lift I needed. I knew I needed to workout and it had to be a good one, so I could think clearly again. My son and I headed out to pick up the girls from school and then we went to the gym.

After a much needed workout, I began to feel a little more normal. I knew what I wanted to do next. I wanted to pray. I began by praying for myself. I prayed for the emotional strength to get through this. I prayed that my children would be understanding while mommy was sad. I prayed for my father's physical and emotional healing. And, I prayed for my mother's strength as she navigated through this horrible experience. Then I shifted into gratitude for their overall well being. The truth is, I was grateful that it wasn't worse. My father was alive. As I started to close out my prayer time, I felt incomplete. Suddenly, I was shocked to realize I wanted to pray for the two men that did this to my daddy. I prayed that whatever pain they must have gone through in their lives to feel the need to hurt a seventy-year-old man in such a violent manner, be healed. I knew if they were healed, this wouldn't happen again.

Later that evening, my sister called me to give me an update. She explained that my dad was still at the hospital waiting on results of a CT Scan of his head. The doctors reported that other than his nose, nothing else on his face had severe damage. It was the swelling that made everything look much worse than it actually was. But then she told me that at the end of her call with our daddy, he asked her if she had seen the latest episode of our favorite TV show. In that moment, I was so relieved because that was a very normal question for my dad to ask, even in a time of duress! I felt like he was telling us "they didn't break me, I am still the father you know and love." I also believe he knew we needed to hear that.

Over the next week or so, the outpouring of love for my father was incredible. Neighbors came out in the storm to check on him and bring over food. My cousins went to visit and I received texts, calls and emails about how inspiring my father's attitude has been since the incident. He healed in record time. In fact, by the time I was able to visit him two weeks later, there were barely any visible signs of the violence on his face. Rather, his face was a beautiful sight to see.

TIME

Out of this painful situation, there was definitely some good. I feel so fortunate to have gotten such a deep look into my father's character. I had always known he was strong, but to watch his inner and outer strength in action through such adversity, is etched in my heart forever. I enjoyed witnessing the love he gives out, come right back to him. People showed up for him because he shows up for people.

I also feel blessed to have learned that I can rise above anger and pain in order to see the "bigger picture" - - that the world needs more *love*. I could have easily submitted to the inhumanity of the two perpetrators. I could have kept my mind locked and loaded on the idea that these two men are bad and, thus, unworthy of love and healing. But if *all* people are born worthy, then that includes those two men. Somewhere along the way, they were misguided and lost sight of their true nature. Until it is restored, they will continue their unacceptable behavior. As such, I pray for their healing so they can stop hurting people. If that ain't love, I don't know what is!

It certainly took some effort to see it this way and not stay stuck on the negative. Too many people stay stuck and it perpetuates throughout our precious world. Maybe I'm an optimist. Maybe I believe in the power of love a little too much. Perhaps! But the one thing I know is that I am on a team of change agents making this world a better place. I was able to rise above a deep rooted pain, involving one of the people I love the most in this world, to maintain my status on that world-changing team. If it's possible for me to do this, I believe that ability lies within each and everyone of us.

LOVE

"Trauma is any stressor that occurs in a sudden and forceful way and is experienced as overwhelming." (*A Healing Journey,* Stephanie Covington) Trauma can take many forms according to the Substance Abuse and Mental Health Services Administration (www.samhsa.gov):

- Sexual abuse or assault
- Physical abuse or assault
- Emotional Abuse or Psychological Maltreatment
- Neglect
- Serious Accident, Illness, or Medical Procedure
- Victim or Witness to Domestic Violence
- Victim or Witness to Community Violence
- Historical Trauma
- School Violence
- Bullying
- Natural or Manmade Disasters
- Forced Displacement
- War, Terrorism, or Political Violence
- Military Trauma

❦ Victim or Witness to Extreme Personal or Interpersonal Violence

❦ Traumatic Grief or Separation

❦ System-Induced Trauma and Re-traumatization

It is important to recognize that you do not have to be the actual recipient of these, to experience them as trauma. While it was my father who was attacked, many others were deeply affected by the incident. When our loved ones go through something traumatic, it can become a "stressor," which simply put, is an event that causes stress. The depth of relationship with the loved one, usually dictates how stressed or overwhelmed we become.

Trauma is a major trigger and we must be aware of the actions that get us back to our mean when it affects us. It doesn't matter how long it takes to process the emotions, stress or pain, it just matters that we are intentionally working on it. I have quite a bit of "practice" getting back to my mean so I knew what to try first. Working out, praying and being with my children are all methods I use to process my feelings when triggered by trauma. In this case, I successfully left the white-knuckled angry person behind and got back to me.

What are some ways you process your emotions, stress and/or pain from trauma?

1. _____
2. _____
3. _____
4. _____
5. _____
6. _____
7. _____
8. _____
9. _____
10. _____

Note: Have these options readily available to you at all times so that you are prepared when adversity strikes. You may need to try one or more, depending on the severity of the blow!

The story about my dad also illustrates the concept of *Divine Order - - God's arrangement of things, in relation to each other, according to a particular sequence, pattern or method, for your highest good.* When we can see things for what they are, how they are and why they've come to be, then we become aware of Divine Order.

Divine Order is recognizable at a micro level and a macro level. For example, you donate a large sum of money to a charity and the next day you receive a refund check from your insurance company. This would be considered at the micro level because you connect the dots quickly and notice the "arrangement" of the events fairly easily.

At the macro level, it will be a more complex arrangement and take us longer to connect the dots. Especially when a lot of time has elapsed between events or when there are those, what I call, *"Where was God When?"* moments.

This experience with my father, was one of those moments. A moment that I couldn't make any sense of, couldn't see the pattern in and certainly couldn't see God's hand in.

These moments challenge us to stay grounded in what we believe, what we know, who we are and who's on our team!

Here are just a few of the realizations that let me know all was in Divine Order:

- My father passed out as a result of bearing attacked, in a blizzard, and yet he woke up.
- A woman happened to be walking by and she chose to help him.
- Airline tickets to visit my dad were very pricey but I knew I wanted to see him right away. When I explained this to my best friend, she just happened to have some "extra" money to lend me.
- I had asked my cousins to go check in on my parents but they couldn't make it right away due to the inclement weather. In the interim, without prompting, their neighbors tended to them.
- My love and appreciation for my dad grew even greater than I thought it could.

Sometimes seeing how things were arranged for us will take some digging along with patience, understanding and perseverance. As tempting as it may be to abandon the search, it's important to recognize that your life lesson is at the other end of it. And your life lessons are where your gifts lie.

So, what if you went searching for your gifts in any given situation? What if you asked yourself *"why is this happening for me?"* each time a challenge arises? This is the most powerful way to approach even your most adverse experiences, because answering this question forwards you. It gives you new awareness about yourself, and about life, that will undoubtedly support you in living from your *mean*.

Chapter 3

Grew Up Atheist and Married a Minister

"If it's true beauty lies in the eye of the beholder
I want my life and what's inside to give Him something to behold
I want a heart that's captivating
I wanna hear my Father saying...
Has anybody told you you're beautiful?
You might agree if you could see what I see"
- Beautiful For Me, A song by Nichole Nordeman

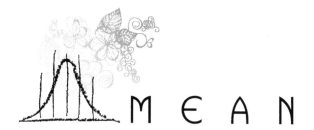 M E A N

I was just finishing up a workshop I presented at a conference for foster parents. I was so inspired. It was such an honor to bring my body of work to this population of people that play such a significant role in our world. Participants were openly sharing their challenges, their pains, their successes and their celebrations associated with fostering children, so openly and authentically. From gay couples conveying the significance of being able to raise children together, to mothers sharing the hurtful struggles they're having with their teen daughters, to men in tears when sharing their fears, it was all beautiful. The energy in the room was electric! You could feel the transformation.

Afterwards, the room was abuzz and people were stopping by to thank me. I was enjoying friendly chatter and big hugs, when suddenly, I felt a shift in the energy. The crowd had dissipated and an elderly woman made her way over to me. She started with a simple request "May I ask you some questions?," to which I obliged. She darted her eyes at me and I no longer felt like I was in the loving environment our group had just spent hours creating. In a condescending tone, she continued with "How old are you young lady?" I shared my age and she paused. She was speaking very slowly yet pointedly as she was intentionally trying to make me feel uneasy. Next she asks me "Where did you get all this?" It was an open ended question and I wasn't exactly sure what she meant but I did my best to answer it when she raised her voice and asserts, "You got this from God!" Although I was losing my patience, at this point I thought I knew where she was coming from and I jumped right in to say "Yes, of course, God was with me through it all..." only to be interrupted again. "Do you go to church?!" to which I responded "Yes, in fact, my husband is a minister." "Do you even read the Bible? Do you know this stuff you are teaching is right there in the Bible!" I couldn't keep up with her questions but it didn't matter. I realized she was trying to make a point and was not interested in a conversation. "Do you believe homosexuality is wrong?" and her look turned into one of disdain when I said "No." She took a longer pause and at this point, I was done with the conversation. As I was about to excuse myself she takes her knuckle and presses it hard against my chest and says "God spoke to me right there" and then she pressed even harder. I slumped my chest inward to ease the pressure. She continued to explain how God let her know that she must evangelize and help people, such as myself, get saved.

Usually, I can brush off people's differing beliefs pretty easily but for some reason this one stopped me in my tracks. I suddenly became very aware that we were the only two people left in the room and I did not want to be there. I finally excused myself and left the room.

I was shocked by her behavior but I was more annoyed than anything. I wasn't sure which bothered me more, the physical violation or the persecution of my beliefs. How dare she! As I walked away, I was rubbing my chest as if to clean her touch off me. I wanted nothing to do with her.

Later on that night, I went to dinner with a colleague of mine who had attended the workshop. I was able to process my feelings about the experience and eventually I got over it. We went on to celebrate my job well done.

TIME

This experience caused me to reflect on my own spiritual growth. You see, I grew up learning atheist beliefs and now I'm married to a minister. As you can imagine, I've undergone quite an evolution.

Anytime someone stirs up such a visceral reaction in you, 9.9 times out of 10, it is triggering something within you that is coming up for attention. A quote by Reverend Sarah Lammert describes this situation perfectly, *"There's something about you I don't like about me."* The woman's behavior and actions got under my skin because she reminded me of how I used to be!

I remember being just as adamant about my beliefs and although I never put my hands on anybody, I certainly hurt some people. You see, growing up armed with atheist beliefs, I was convinced there was no God and religion served no purpose but to control people. It seemed anyone I shared this with would challenge me and the thing is, I love to "win" challenges. I would try to convince them I was right and, unfortunately, in pursuit of that win, I trampled on peoples' beliefs as well as their feelings. I was completely out of alignment with my true nature. It took some serious self-forgiveness to let myself off the hook from my behavior back then.

I learned that it actually takes way more energy to go against our true nature than to go with the flow of it. I recall being exhausted, frustrated and defensive, all the time. Exactly how it feels to suppress your authenticity. It wasn't until I got honest about my spiritual beliefs, that I freed myself from this pain and opened myself up to a new kind of love - - not just with God but with my husband the Minister!

 LOVE

The woman who approached me after the workshop, came into my life to teach me several things. For starters, she reminded me that it is more powerful to embody your spiritual beliefs than to try to shove them down someones throat. By being my spirituality, I was able to remain calm, hear her out and kindly excuse myself as soon as the opportunity presented itself rather than engage in a debate that would get us nowhere good. I demonstrated key attributes of my spiritual beliefs - - love and acceptance. Sometimes we don't have to say a word and our presence sends the memo.

She also showed me how far I've come in the process of self-love. Had I not been absolutely clear about who I am; 100% in love with who I am; and unapologetically willing to express who I am; in all honesty, I would have flipped my lid at the first sign of her aggressive behavior. I would have showed up in a way that does not reflect my true nature because that is what I was used to doing when triggered by someone's negative opinions, behaviors or actions.

Now is a good time to explore the concept of *overcompensating*. In simple terms, overcompensating means taking excessive measures to make amends for an error, weakness or problem (www.dictionary.com). In the context of self-love, even though you have forgiven yourself for the error, weakness or problem you caused, you are afraid of awakening inauthentic behavior from your past. As a result, you respond in a way that contrasts that old behavior but it ends up being detrimental as well. While you may not have unleashed the prior negative behavior, you will still find yourself out of alignment with your authentic self just in a different way.

For example, a woman has a tendency to interrupt her co-workers during team meetings. Eventually she finds out that people think she is rude and inconsiderate. From that point forward, she overcompensates by holding back at meetings and not sharing her input. Authentically she wants to participate but she is too afraid of being negatively perceived. The *authentic action* would be to acknowledge her behavior and do the inner work it takes to be effective at the meetings.

This idea of overcompensating does not stem from a feeling of unworthiness, rather, it stems from fear of falling back into an old, inauthentic version of yourself that no longer represents who you choose to be and how you choose to show up.

Over the years, I've realized that sometimes I get afraid of unleashing my "old self" when someone has disrespected or hurt me. I've conquered this fear when dealing with people I don't have a relationship with, as in the case with the woman at the workshop. These situations aren't much of a trigger for me anymore because the wound doesn't go deep and I can easily process my emotions.

It's a different story when it's someone I am in relationship with whether that be my intimate partner, family or friends. There are more feelings vested and more at stake. As is human nature, I want to feel loved, appreciated and respected by them. When it doesn't feel that way, depending on the level of discord, my emotions can get out of control.

As I mentioned earlier, the "old" Anita would feel hurt or dis-respected and instantly react. My mouth was my weapon and I was astute at hitting people where it hurts with my words. While it is rare, there are times I do backslide into this behavior which I will explore more throughout this chapter and into the next one. But there are also times when I retreat to the opposite corner. I let people get away with offensive behavior because I don't want to react so adversely. I don't want to lose control and step out of alignment with myself so drastically. As a result, I've ended up giving people license to dishonor me which has felt just as disappointing and has required just as much processing as losing control of my temper.

In essence, overcompensating equates to inauthentic behavior that will require your love and attention to get back on track.

Let's explore this idea of backsliding. When we react to a situation based on our emotions, rather than take the time needed to respond to it authentically, an outdated pattern has kicked in. *Outdated patterns* are old beliefs, thoughts, or behaviors that no longer serve you and are playing out in your life. These are either hard to detect or you are aware of them and you are working on putting an end to their influence.

In either case, you have momentarily stepped out of alignment with your *mean*. I call this, *drifting* - - veering off your authentic path. The length of time you're "out there" and the ensuing repercussions, will vary according to your mastery of reconnecting with your authentic self.

As you drift, you run the risk of a snowball effect on your consequences. I call it the *Tap-Knock-Crash*. Here is how it works:

The Tap: You receive a gentle message that it is time for you to shift back into alignment with your authentic self.

> ❦ Whether the message came through meditation, contemplation or inner discovery, you have been informed that it is time for a change and you listen and comply. The risk ends there.

The Knock: It comes if you don't adhere to the Tap. It is a stronger, louder, even obnoxious, message indicating it's time for you to shift.

> ❦ It comes in a more jolting, surprising, scary or annoying manner and you must break through stuckness, stubbornness or "knowing it all" in order to listen and comply. By this point you've paid prices.

The Crash: The Tap and Knock did not get through to you. The crash is a rock bottom moment that gives you no alternative but to change!

🥀 It is a strong, obvious and extremely painful experience that forces you to shift. You have lost control of the situation and have no where to go but up.

The majority of people who haven't achieved self-love, or at least started the journey, are in the drift whether they are conscious of it or not. The drift is comfortable and familiar even if it's painful! Getting out of the drift requires a conscious awakening into discovery of who you are, what it means to love yourself and having the courage to be yourself. It is ideal for this awakening to occur at the Tap stage but, obviously, that is not always the case. While I am grateful for my rock bottom moment because that is when I turned my life around, I don't wish that level of trauma on anyone.

The following are some red-flags that you are drifting:

🥀 *You are running on auto-pilot* - Not putting intentional thought behind your behaviors and actions.

🥀 *You are avoiding challenges* - Not addressing barriers that are in your way of extraordinary living.

🥀 *You are making a lot of excuses and placing blame on others* - Unwilling to look within for your way forward.

🥀 *You are experiencing more downs than ups* - Spending more time in breakdown than moving in the direction of your dreams.

🥀 *You are stagnant* - Not necessarily in breakdown but you are not moving forward.

If you find yourself stuck, you may have some release work to do. *To release* is to free yourself from the emotional attachment to someone, some thing [an idea, thought] or some experience.

Here are five powerful steps for releasing outdated patterns:

1. **Get clear on, or reacquaint yourself with, your vision for your life.**
    The vision for your life, in all areas, must be your driving force. In *Mean Time Love: A Woman's Journey From Self-Loathe to Self-Love*, I provide detailed worksheets that support you in developing your vision in these key areas: *Spirituality, Intimate Relationship, Family, Friendship, Career, Finances, Health, Education and Community*. If you've lost sight of your vision, feel free to revisit these worksheets so that you can get crystal clear. Let's face it, there will be days you won't want to do the work! Your motivation for achieving your dreams must triumph over the comfort of staying stuck.

2. **Answer the question, "Why Am I holding on?"**
    Explore what you believe you're gaining from sticking to the old belief, thought or behavior so that you can identify what you are afraid of losing, if you were to let it go.

3. **Make a conscious choice to release it.**
    When you are crystal clear that you get to let go of this outdated pattern in order to achieve your dreams, make the choice to let it go. Say it, write it and/or tell a friend.

4. **Process your emotions.**
    Honor your feelings. Give yourself the opportunity to feel how you feel. Be sure not to stuff them somewhere as they will eventually show up again and it's usually in an even unhealthier manner than the first go around. Use the tools you have to get grounded in you and heal, if necessary, so that you can break free from the influence of the outdated pattern.

5. **Be ready and available to celebrate your success!**
   The net result will be extraordinary because you did the work to get there. Be ready for it and don't forget to give yourself kudos for doing this work. Breaking an outdated pattern is a serious accomplishment!

Chapter 4

It's Not About the Dishes

"Say it to me now
Say it to me anyway
Everything your heart would say
If all the walls came down
Say it to me now
Even if the truth tears us apart
I need to feel the closeness
Of knowing what's in your heart"
- Say It To Me Now, A song by Beth Nielsen Chapman

 M E A N

My husband and I were in the thick of an argument. He left his dirty dishes somewhere they didn't belong, for what felt like the millionth time. In previous discussions about this issue, I had explained to him that it makes me feel like he "expects" me to clean up after him. He would always assure me that wasn't the case and commit to doing better. Yet here we were again.

Most people would be able to keep their cool and work through this calmly. Not me, I could feel the anger building up. It started with a dull pain in my heart, turned into a sharp one and then my mind took over, all within seconds. My mind takes over because, for years, I trained my heart not to sit in pain. Apparently, not even for a second. I was trying my best to hold it in. I really didn't want to completely lose it. I never do. I know better. Even in my blind anger, I could hear myself saying *"give yourself time to feel your feelings and respond when you have processed them."* It was something I taught often but right now, in the heat of the moment, I was struggling to practice what I preached.

His voice became muffled in the background of my racing mind and there I went. Completely over the edge. I started screaming at the top of my lungs. I got defensive, offensive and adrenaline ridden...over some dishes. He completely shut down, disengaged and eventually walked away, which only made me more upset.

After he left, I started to cry. I was disappointed in myself and sad that I hurt my husband. I literally regretted each second I was in that escalated state. I began to think about how I got there. Why did the dirty dishes bother me so much?

Once I did the inner work to seek understanding, I realized the dishes represented feeling unheard, unseen and taken for granted. Feelings I've had in many of my past intimate relationships and rather than use proven methods for working through these feelings in a healthy manner, I was triggered.

After a few hours of retreating to our "corners," we came together to talk. I apologized for my behavior and my inability to articulate my feelings effectively. I acknowledged the work I get to do to break the pattern of this "zero to sixty" temper. I explained it was not how I want to show up, especially with him. I went on to let him know how awful it felt to be so disappointed in myself. He had not yet gotten to the place where he could feel compassion but he listened, and he accepted my apology.

As he reflected, he realized he couldn't commit to always putting his dirty dishes away. Somedays he might not get it right, but he did commit to doing his best to make me feel loved, appreciated and understood. That worked for me.

TIME

Whoever said that being married is like having a mirror to your face everyday, was not kidding! I have always maintained that if it wasn't for the love my husband and I share, I simply would not do the "work" of a marriage. By work, I mean the act of being vulnerable - - expressing your authentic self - - even when you feel profoundly hurt or afraid. Love creates a safe space for us to be vulnerable. I find it easy to express myself when the conditions, or situation, is to my liking. I'm tested when the circumstances are uncomfortable or painful.

I will not lie, it was hard for me, the *"self-love coach,"* to realize I still had some deep rooted issues causing me to behave in such an extreme manner - - so far from my mean. And coming to this realization within the context of my intimate relationship only exacerbated things. It's one thing to recognize something you don't like about yourself behind closed doors, but for it to unfold in front of someone you hold in such high regard...well that's just no fun. That's when ego steps in and I start caring more about how I look than effectively communicating my feelings. Don't get me wrong, that is the ego's job. It's main purpose is to keep us looking good at any cost. The problem is that, most of the time, it operates erroneously. In my case I needed to "win" the argument. Be the loudest. Never surrender. Be the last woman standing. Make my hurt go away at all costs. But that was so far from simply wanting to be heard, seen and valued. The truth is, I lost. My authentic self got sidelined and my emotions ran the show. I was out there winging it with my outdated ways and ended up hurting someone I love.

An intimate relationship worth working for will continually stretch you. It will continually point you within. It will continually show you more of who you are. The key is that the relationship must continue to be worth it. It must continue to be healthy for you. It must continue to *supplement* your life.

At the point when you've achieved your mean, there are three potential states you can be in as it pertains to intimate relationship:

1. *You have released an unhealthy intimate relationship (or relationships depending on the length of your journey) and are rebuilding your confidence to enter into a new one.* - This is a direct result of recognizing that your partner's actions and behaviors did not align with your innate worth and this was

no longer acceptable in your experience. So even if it hurts to let them go, you follow through and do so. However, you are aware that you need time to build the confidence in expressing your authentic self at this level of intimacy before re-engaging in the dating process.

2. *You have chosen to take your current relationship to a new level of authenticity.* - The love you share with your partner is strong enough to sustain your personal growth and you will, unprecedentedly, share your authentic self with them. Your partner is open to learning, loving and accepting the "new" you. The number one question I get from people who are on this self-love journey is "Can I do this while I'm in a relationship?" I always say yes, it is possible, you will need time to yourself for discovery and both persons must be open to change. In other words, if you are growing, so must your partner.

3. *You are open to having an intimate relationship.* - You have achieved a level of mastery in expressing your authentic self and are ready to fully share yourself with someone else.

In any of these scenarios, it is important to understand and embrace the key distinctions of a thriving intimate relationship because they lay a foundation strong enough to persevere through the most stubborn triggers. Here is what it requires of each individual:

🌹 *An awareness that they are perfect, whole and complete.*
It is in this awareness that you and your partner define the relationship rather than be defined by the relationship. You can co-create the relationship of your dreams when you understand what you bring to the table. On the

other hand, when you feel less than, unworthy or broken, you run the risk of being in the relationship for the wrong reasons which leads to unhealthy outcomes - - misunderstandings, codependency, false expectations, infidelity, among others.

🌹 *Unconditional love.*
You are accepting, forgiving, patient, compassionate and kind with each other. You appreciate your partner and you do not judge them. You don't always agree with their choices but you will align with them if it is their true desire. You seek understanding but it is not a condition for your love. I don't pretend to understand why my husband can't put away his dishes when I find it to be an easy task for me. I choose to love him anyway. He doesn't understand how I go from zero to sixty in seconds and, yet, he loves me anyway.

🌹 *Vulnerability*
Vulnerable in the context of sharing your authentic self with your partner no matter how scary or uncomfortable it may be, as opposed to the more common definition of leaving yourself open to attack. Being vulnerable is not to be mistaken for sharing your emotions because emotions are temperamental and can lead us astray. You will be able to decipher what it is you wish to express, once you have processed your emotions. You may rock the boat in speaking your truth and it may even cause a hurdle for you to get through but in a thriving relationship, the work is worth it. At the end of the day, being vulnerable is one of the most powerful ways your partner can see you and learn about you.

❦ *Communication such that the other person gets it*
If you are talking a language that your partner doesn't speak then you are simply talking to yourself. In a thriving relationship, you are willing to take the time, and put forth the effort, to ensure your partner understands the information you are seeking to convey to them. It may take multiple attempts, and creativity, depending on the complexity and sensitivity of the topic. If the first attempt doesn't work, then go back to the drawing board and come up with another way. Everyone learns, interprets and comprehends in different ways. You can't take for granted that they will "get it" simply because they are your partner.

❦ *A conscious choosing of each other.*
You are with your partner simply because you want to be. You are not with them because:

- ❦ It is your duty.
- ❦ Your mom, dad, grandmother, grandfather or anyone you hold in high esteem, wants you to be with them.
- ❦ Society says you should be with them.
- ❦ You're afraid of leaving them.
- ❦ You feel guilty about leaving them.
- ❦ You're obligated to be with them.
- ❦ You're the only one who can save them.
- ❦ You'll regret not being with them.
- ❦ You may love them one day.
- ❦ Or any combination thereof.

Let's face it, we can't live with intimate relationships and we can't live without them! But what we can do is ensure that we are in it for the right reasons; that it is truly supplemental to our lives; and that we are enjoying the ride.

⸎⸎⸎ ON REJECTION... ⸎⸎⸎

As you can tell, engaging in intimate relationship, from your mean, requires you to share yourself in an unfiltered way. Because of the level of closeness involved and the desire to maintain it, any inkling of rejection can be painful. In times of disagreements, unreciprocated feelings or experiences of "conditional" love, it is important to navigate feelings of rejection effectively. We must decipher what is true and what we make up about a situation. Then it is up to us to align our choices, behaviors and actions with the truth.

Rejection is a feeling not fact. Something happens that triggers us to feel separate from someone or something we care about. The facts are what actually happened, to trigger the emotions. Emotions are a natural consequence and are meant to be processed. That's it! Don't let it go any further than that. Don't let your mind run away with all types of false, negative thoughts about yourself.

It brings to mind a time when I was very excited about returning to a conference for a fourth year in a row. It was an amazing conference aimed at supporting teen girls that were at risk for being sexually exploited. I had fallen in love with these girls and the multiple opportunities to be in the conversation of self-love with them. Well to my surprise, I was not invited back that year and all of my attempts to communicate with the planning team were just that, attempts. Not one response. I couldn't believe it because we had established such a great rapport. I really wanted to return so this hurt. I started to wonder if they had found someone better or younger. I was second guessing my performance from previous years. My thoughts were all over the place, none of which were positive. After licking my wounds and processing my feelings, I finally released the emotional attachment I had to being at the conference. At that point of clarity, I came to the conclusion that it was time for the girls to have a new experience with other speakers and it was my time to move on to my next project.

The best way to deal with rejection is to see it as a gateway to your next opportunity. If someone or something isn't for us, there is someone or something else out there for us. No authentic effort goes unanswered, so your only job is to stay authentic in all areas of your life.

Chapter 5

The Big C

"Sometimes you wanna run away
Ain't got the patience for the pain
And if you don't believe it
look into your heart
The beat goes on
I'm tellin' you things get better through whatever
If you fall, dust it off, don't let up
Don't you know you can go be your own miracle
You need to know!
If the mind keeps thinking you've had enough
But the heart keeps telling you 'don't give up'
Who are we to be questioning, wondering what is what?
Don't give up, through it all, just stand up."
- Just Stand Up, A song by Artists Stand Up to Cancer

MEAN

was nine months pregnant with my son and I was finally slowing down. Up to that point, as if raising a one and a two year old wasn't enough, I was also speaking, facilitating retreats and doing book events quite often. My career was finally taking off. But now it was time for me to relax and listen to my body. Even though I wanted to ride the momentum of my success, I knew it was time to take a load off. It was evident by the fact that at that point, I could hardly walk. One day, as I tried to get comfortable at my desk, I decided to tackle a large pile of paperwork that had recently piled up. As I sorted through it, I stumbled upon an invitation to a luncheon by a group called Circle of Promise - - an organization that raises awareness of breast cancer, particularly to the African American community due to the disproportionately high death rate of African American women from this disease. It looked like something I definitely wanted to get involved in, but this particular luncheon was occurring the week of my due date. So I marked it as something I will address post-baby and put it aside.

I spent the first several months of my son's life tending to his every need and getting my arms around how I was going to balance three children, my marriage and my career. While I successfully put "work" aside as long as I could, it was time for me to get back into action. Top of my list, was contacting Circle of Promise to see how I could serve.

I got an immediate response asking me to come in and present all of my services to their group. I was so excited because I was being given an opportunity to reach a new demographic of women and breast cancer awareness is such an important cause. I just didn't realize how important it was about to become…to me.

It was time to do my research and the first thing I did was interview a close friend of mine who is a breast cancer survivor. As she told me her story from diagnosis to double mastectomy to becoming a survivor, my love for her grew deeper with each tear that crawled down her cheek and each word she spoke that landed on my heart. At the end of the conversation, I asked her, "What got you through such a challenging time?" She triumphantly shared "I just told myself, I'm not going anywhere!" and continued to tell me how she persistently did "everything in her power to survive." That was just what I needed to hear to connect the dots of how self-love plays a significant role in the will to survive such a horrific disease.

I realized that I wanted women to love themselves enough to be proactive about their breast health and whether it is going for a mammogram, getting a diagnosis, living with breast cancer or being a survivor, loving themselves through the entire journey. I wanted to encourage women not to let their fears stop them from taking care of themselves. Yes, it is scary to find out you might have to fight for your life but truly believing you have a life worth fighting for, would help you break through the fear.

I also learned that women are afraid of not feeling attractive if their breasts are removed, but "what if they could see their beauty no matter what?"

Prepared with a powerful message, I rocked the presentation to Circle of Promise and they wanted to get started right away. I was asked to submit a grant proposal to Susan G. Komen - - who approves the funding for such programs - - for facilitating a retreat for African American women in the Sacramento area, that would ultimately boost proactive breast care. Again, I was beyond excited.

Three weeks later, I found out that the proposal was not approved, but they assured me they would research other ways for us to work together.

Months had passed and while Circle of Promise was still on my radar, I was busy with other speaking events and, really, just life in general. After all, life must go on. One day my gym buddy, Ceonita, and I had just finished our very fun Zumba class - - a cardio dance workout - - and we were headed to the gym floor for some strength training. Among our normal workout chatter, she stops me in my tracks with, "By the way, I have breast cancer." I looked at her and, immediately, felt tears welling up. She looked back at me and said, "No, you don't get to cry. If I'm not crying, you don't get to cry." This was tough for me because I'm a "crier" but I certainly didn't want to make this about me, so I pulled myself together. For a while, we pretended to lift weights as we talked about how she found out and how she's been coping with the news. It turned out, even though we worked out together just about everyday, she didn't tell me about her biopsy until the results came in. My gym buddy has a great sense of humor and a perspective on life that is light and refreshing, so it was natural for her to start joking about the situation. However, I was not ready for the jokes so I asked her if I could take 24 hours to process my feelings and get back to her. Of course, she understood.

The reality was that my friend, who's the same age as I am, has two small children, is loved by so many and could give you 20 pushups in the blink of an eye, had cancer. I knew she was about to embark on a challenging journey and I decided I was going to be there for her every step of the way.

The first thing I did, was organize a Zumbathon to take place on the day of Ceo's double mastectomy because I knew it was something she loved to do. In the weeks leading up to this big day, we announced it at the gym and asked everyone to wear pink in honor of breast cancer awareness. I even made 100 pink ribbon lapel pins. This was so out of character for me because "crafts" were not my thing. Just to get what I needed, I went to a crafts store and asked 5 different people about 4 million questions. By the time I left the store the staff were cheering me on and assuring me I could do it! It took a lot of focus, attention to detail and holding my little curious children at bay, to make those ribbons.

So while my gym buddy was having both of her breasts, a stage two lump of cancer and several lymph nodes removed from her body, her friends and I, danced harder than we've ever danced. Some of us prayed in between songs. Some of us had cards prepared and we even shot a video greeting her and wishing her well. She loved it!

I went on to visit her right after her surgery. As I walked in and handed her a bunch of fun gifts, I was caught off guard by the drains attached to her body that were removing excess fluids from the surgical site. She was moving slow and up to that point, I didn't even know she was capable of that. But I quickly became aware that none of this had "broken" her. She was still the same positive, hilarious, fun Ceo that I know and love. We cracked a few jokes and talked a bit before she needed to go lay down.

When it was time to start chemotherapy, she met with her oncologist and was confronted with what she called a 'test of her faith.' The doctor opened their discussion with "you have a 50/50 chance of survival from here" and had an "oh poor baby" approach. This was not even close to anything in my friend's experience up to that point and while she held it together during the appointment, for the first time since this challenge began, she cried when she left the office. When Ceo told me about this encounter, I let her know "this oncologist is just not your style, let's go ahead and kindly decline her services." In the moment she seemed hesitant but a couple days later, Ceo had a new oncologist. One that had an attitude more aligned with her own.

I made her food from recipes she selected out of a "healing cancer" cookbook and dropped it off at her house a couple of times over the course of her recovery. She's so loved, I was certainly not the only one, but I did my part.

I got myself on her schedule as one of her drivers for chemo sessions. I took her to a couple of different sessions spread out over a couple of months. We laughed, talked and ate not-so-good hospital food before she fell asleep. Sometimes I would work or read a magazine while she slept and sometimes I just watched her. She looked so beautiful, and peaceful, curled up in a large chair that engulfed her small frame, as harsh chemicals were being pumped into her body. Harsh chemicals that would ultimately save her life, despite any other illusion the purple fingernails, loss of hair, severe nausea and intermittently fatigued body, would attempt to insinuate.

She got to a point where she knew the "chemo" cycle. She would basically be home for the first week after treatment, either nauseous or sleeping, and by the second week she could come out and play a little bit. We would do light workouts or just hangout. Then it was time for her next round of chemo.

After chemo, she handled radiation like a champ! Most people would complain about having to be at a hospital every day of the week, but not Ceo. Even with her very busy life, she was where she needed to be, when she needed to be there.

As I went on this journey with her, I got so inspired that I wrote an email to Circle of Promise. I wanted to let them know that I was now prepared to do some pro bono work with them whether it be the retreat we previously discussed, a workshop, a keynote, it didn't matter! The money was no longer as important as the cause. At that very moment, one of my children needed something from me, so I stopped what I was doing and didn't send the email just yet. I saved it in my Drafts folder and went on with my day.

Within two hours, I received an email from Circle of Promise saying that they've allocated funding to have me come in and facilitate a four-hour workshop at one of their all day conferences…and I hadn't even sent them my email!

TIME

Today, my friend is cancer free! The thing that amazed me the most was Ceonita's attitude. From the day she found out she had breast cancer, she had been so positive. Never doubting for a minute that she will win this battle! In an email she wrote to a couple of her close friends explaining the situation, she wrote, *"The fact I have cancer…uh its stage 2 early and treatable. Totally pumped I can get it out, over and done with. I compare my treatment plan to a scene in a movie where the hero shoots the villain and then for good measure pops him a few more times in the head."* Basically, she was clear about what she needed to do and she was going to be herself, through it all.

This was a game-changer for me. I had never seen someone handle such a life-changing experience with such ease, grace and humor. And to be honest, at the beginning I thought it was a cover up. I thought, perhaps, this was the face she was showing the world and on the inside, she was sad, scared or simply not so optimistic. I learned quickly, as our friendship grew deeper, that this is who she is authentically. To this day, she is one of my greatest inspirations and reminders that attitude changes everything.

Ceonita's refreshing attitude made it so much easier for me to shift out of my feelings about the situation and into Champion mode. There was a part of me that initially wanted to submit to fear. I could have easily recited every possible scenario of doom and gloom but I genuinely didn't have those thoughts. As a result, I was able to be who she wanted me to be on the journey and I enjoyed every minute of it.

LOVE

In addition to the powerful inspiration I draw from this experience, there are a few lessons that stand out.

First, is the distinction between "losing" your identity and expanding your understanding of yourself. As we venture into the unknown, we are presented with the opportunities to access new aspects, or dormant aspects, of ourselves. This can seem foreign and at times, we may question whether we are staying true to ourselves. The key is that the choice you make is authentic, then the particulars of the new experience will reveal more about who you are.

For example, when I chose to make the 100 pink ribbon lapel pins, I was out of my comfort zone particularly because I had no idea what I was doing. The key to my success was that I was passionate about *why* I was making them. As a result, I learned that I am capable of doing crafts projects and this has become important in my life now that my children love such projects.

Life will continue to happen and, as my friend Curtis Dennis of

Momentum Education says, the world will keep "worlding." All the while, defining moments will mold us along the way. It's our responsibility to consciously evolve through these experiences so that we don't wake up one day wondering who's identity we've assumed. It's so important to schedule time to check in with ourselves. *We get to re-acquaint ourselves with ourselves, on an ongoing basis.*

As you look within, you want to consider the following ways we identify ourselves and how they have been impacted by defining moments in your life:

🌹 Your intrinsic ways of being

🌹 How you show up in the world

🌹 What you stand for, and

🌹 What you emanate into the world (Your energy)

When Ceonita switched doctors, she knew she wasn't about to drop in consciousness to meet the level of the "negative" oncologist. Even if what the doctor was saying was statistically true, Ceonita knew this person was not a match. Her choice to release this doctor made room for the right and perfect doctor to be on her team.

Stay true to who you are and the gifts will come! In choosing to be there for my friend through her battle with cancer, I did a lot of new things, walked new walks and had quite a few "firsts," all of which broadened my understanding of who I am but the greatest gift was the nurturing of a friendship that means the world to me.

When I moved to Sacramento, I had no family other than my husband and children. No one else that I could completely unwind with, trust my children with, or even, my life with. Now I do. If the tables were turned, Ceonita would be there for me.

I've inadvertently learned that nurturing a friendship is worth the effort, especially if it doesn't feel like an effort.

I've encountered so many women that feel lonely because they don't have healthy relationships. Never underestimate the power of making a new friend. Simply get intentional about building friendships that are authentic, meaningful, reciprocal and steeped in love.

My husband, Reverend Kevin Kitrell Ross, says "INTENTION + ATTENTION = MANIFESTATION." If you decide you want to have meaningful friendships then choose to make it happen. There is power in your choice! Once you make the choice, give it some attention. Take action! Go to new places, events, meet ups, churches, volunteer opportunities or organizations where you will find people with similar interests. Then be open with them. Show them who you are, like, for real! The only way to attract authentic relationships is to be authentic. From there, I like to say, the "magic" will happen - - the beauty of friendship will evolve in your life.

The last lesson I took away from this experience is when something is meant for you, it will manifest in your life. It wasn't my time to work with Circle of Promise, *until it was my time*. I was meant to draw on my personal experience before teaching women how to fight this deadly disease, and thrive in their survival of it.

Four years after my first workshop at Circle of Promise, I encountered a participant who was a breast cancer survivor. She cried in my arms and shared the impact I made on her life that day. I know my personal connection to her experience had a lot to do with the difference I made. *We can't rush the process. Just trust the process.*

Chapter 6

When Lil' Mama Fought Back

"You were my strength when I was weak
You were my voice when I couldn't speak
You were my eyes when I couldn't see
You saw the best there was in me
Lifted me up when I could not reach
You gave me faith because you believed
I am everything I am
Because you loved me"

- Because You Loved Me, A song by Celine Dion

M E A N

I was on a tight schedule as I headed to pick up my daughters from school so I called the school to ask them to get the girls ready and have them wait for me in the lobby. They replied they couldn't do that and proceeded to let me know that I had to come in and talk to the principal. Something had happened to my daughter, Lil' Mama. Not only was this exchange concerning but I had a coaching session at 6:00pm sharp and I was already cutting it close. I tried to explain that

I didn't have much time but they insisted I had to come in and that is when I realized the seriousness of the situation. I was freaking out at this point so I canceled my coaching session, my head was no longer in it anyway.

As soon as I arrived at the school, they scooped my son from me and said they would watch my kiddos while I was taken directly to the Principal's office. As they broke the news to me that an older child said something sexually explicit to my kindergartner and her two friends, I could feel myself slumping in my chair. The boy ended his derogatory comments by letting my daughter know that if she told anyone, she could "get shot and die."

My heart was crushed. My innocent baby. Mommy wasn't there to protect her from this terrible situation. Everyone in the room was extremely emotional. Through my tears I heard them say despite the threatening language, my daughter was the only one to tell a teacher right away. I thought to myself, "that's my brave girl!" They went on to say that she will probably think she is in trouble and that it would be best for me not to show too much emotion as it may scare her.

I pulled myself together and walked outside. First thing she asked me in her littlest voice was "Am I in trouble?" to which I quickly replied "No baby, you're not in trouble. You did everything right. You're amazing!" and I hugged her tightly.

As I loaded my three children in the car, I wondered how I was going to handle this. I didn't know how this would impact her emotionally or if there would be a developmental impact. I knew I had to talk to her without my other children around, which was already no easy task, but on top of that, this was a "mommy first" for me and I was in unchartered territory.

When we got home, I got my daughters settled in to do their homework and my three year old occupied with an interesting toy. I took this opportunity to call my friend who's not only a teacher but always gives me great advice. Together we came up with a game plan for how I would approach this big, tough talk with my little, strong girl.

I called my daughter up to my office and sat her down. First, I asked her "So what happened today?" As she explained pretty much what I heard earlier, I listened intently. I asked her whatever questions I needed for clarity. Next, I told her that this child's behavior was completely unacceptable, inappropriate and disrespectful. She proceeded to say "and it was bad!" to which I promptly agreed. I, then, explained that I have great confidence in her that if something like this should ever happen again, she will know how to handle herself. She looked so proud of herself. I went on to explain that she has power within her and that this child tried to take it from her. Before I could go on she jumped up and said "and I stood up for myself!" I gave her a high five and hugged her so tight. It was an amazing moment for both of us.

Over the next few days, I struggled with my fears about what happened to Lil' Mama. My thoughts kept shifting in and out of my own experiences with gun violence and it magnified her situation in my mind. Because of this, I needed to stay in tune with my daughter and what she needed from me. I wasn't sure if it was best to continue the dialogue with her or let it go. I didn't want to create something that wasn't there for her but only lived on in my thoughts. On top of that, I didn't know whether or not to tell her older sister what happened. I decided to call my friend, a psychologist. After that conversation, I felt good about my next steps.

To my surprise and relief, the whole situation blew over in less than a week.

TIME

I am on high alert with my children. When something happens to them, even an "ouchie" on the playground, I experience a tremor through my body and it actually startles me. Then I go into protection mode. I doubt I am the only mother to have this experience but I do love this aspect of myself. Balancing the need for my children to learn on their own and the demonstration of my deep love for them, is a great feat and I believe one that continually defines, or should I say redefines, me as a mother.

It has taken me some time, and immense growth, to recognize that I cannot protect them from everything but that it is my job to love them through it all. *Love them in a way that allows them to evolve into the person they truly are, not the person that the world seeks to form them into.* Admittedly, there are nights I lose sleep over this assignment, knowing I won't always get it right.

My daughter once told me that she wanted to flatten her pony tail because a girl in her Pre-K class, said she doesn't like "big" hair. Initially, I was angry and defensive because it took me back to similar experiences I had as a child but when I looked in my baby girl's eyes, I knew she needed solutions not anger. So I let my "stuff" go and started by letting her know how beautiful she is, as she is. Then I whipped out my cell phone and searched for a book called *Big Hair Don't Care* by Crystal Swain-Bates.

I showed her the book cover with a beautiful little girl with big curly hair and my daughter looked at me with a smile that meant everything. Of course we ordered the book on the spot and once it was in her hands, she asked me to read it everyday for weeks. She hasn't let anyone else's concerns about her hair affect her, ever since. In fact, she wears her hair confidently in all the beautiful ways, only she can.

I share this story because when we do get it right, it is absolutely triumphant!

 LOVE

It is still a blur how I handled the situation with Lil' Mama given my extreme emotions around what happened to her, but somehow I prevailed through it. At times like this, the deep mental, spiritual and physical strength of a mother bewilders me. Mostly because, in my experience, I feel like it developed overnight. There was a literal shift in me when I became ready for this journey called motherhood. I recall finding a crying baby at a restaurant annoying and then out of nowhere, it wasn't. On the contrary, I would hear a crying baby and be concerned about the little one. I even wanted to help. Then I became a mother and it felt like I tapped into what I like to call, "Mommy Power!"

I witnessed my mother wield these super powers when I was growing up. She worked a full-time 9 to 5 job, rode the subway to and from work with long walks to the stations and managed to have a home cooked meal on the table every night. On top of that, she was very active in her community, in the political process and in the greater fight for social justice. As if that isn't enough she went back to school, later in life, to finish her college degree, while raising two young daughters, so she could further her career and demonstrate what it takes to go for your dreams. All the while, she did everything she knew to do, to raise two independent, intelligent and loving change-agent women.

Well, the apple didn't fall too far from the tree. When my three children were young and still very much dependent on me, my days seemed to never end. Let's just take a peek into a typical day of my life during their early childhood years:

- Wake up at 6:30am and get myself ready for the day.
- Wake the girls up and make sure they get dressed, brush teeth, etc.
- Wake Khaiden up, escort him to potty, get him dressed, help him brush his teeth.
- Pack their lunch, make their breakfast, make their kale smoothies.
- Eat something myself (on a good day)
- Do their hair.
- Put shoes and jackets on, prepare backpacks and we're out the door.
- Pile up in the car and head to the girls' school.
- Drop off girls.
- Drive across town and drop Kaiden off at his pre-school
- Drive to work.
- Accomplish a whole lot at work.
- Change into gym clothes.
- Pick up Khaiden from school.

- Give him a snack.
- Check him into the Kidz Club at the gym.
- Work hard at my Bootcamp class.
- Get Khaiden and head to pick up the girls.
- Get home and start cooking dinner.
- Help them do their homework.
- Eat dinner.
- Bath them, help them brush their teeth, get them ready for bed.
- Read books, pray, lights out.
- Get on my laptop and do some Mean Time Love work.
- Hang out with husband.
- Watch some TV.
- Go to sleep.

Are you exhausted? Can you relate? Do you have, or have you had, similar days? Sometimes, I look at what I've accomplished in a day and say "God, where does the strength come from?!!" Of course, there are also nights I say "God give me the strength!" But the simple answer to this question is that this strength is powered by *love*! I would venture out and say God's love, or love from that which you acknowledge as your higher power. Because, honestly, that love is quite miraculous. My husband constantly asks me when I'm going to slow down and I realize he doesn't get it. It's a mother thing! There isn't anything tangible I can hold on to, or show him, that makes me able to *be* all that I am on a daily basis. It's just love that keeps me going. Love for myself, my babies, my husband, my family and for the world.

One of my favorite definitions of *strength* comes from Charles Filmore's *The Revealing Word*, where he says it is the *"Capac-*

ity to accomplish; Stability of character; Freedom from weakness; Power to withstand temptation. Strength is physical, mental, and spiritual."

This experience with Lil' Mama, inspires me to look at these aspects of strength through a mother's eyes.

Let's start with the *capacity to accomplish*. Mothers are doers, nurturers, caretakers, supporters and so much more. We've already covered what's possible in a day so now I want to share a story I once heard a long time ago as a child. I used to think it was a myth, but it's true. A mother actually lifted a car to save her son's life! What an amazing accomplishment. But now that I'm a mother, I no longer see it as impossible.

In 1982, Anthony Cavallo was underneath his 1964 Chevy Impala when the jack slipped away leaving Anthony clamped between the top of the rear wheel and the fender of a car that was over 3,000 pounds. His mother Angela, who described herself as "5-foot-8, large framed and strong" was in the kitchen when a child from the neighborhood ran in and told her what had happened. Story goes that she ran out, said a prayer then lifted the corner of the car just a few inches so it didn't keep pressing on her son while the kid went to get help. She held the corner of the car for about 5 minutes until help came and pulled her son out. Anthony fully recovered, and today he runs five Goodyear tire stores.

Now that's the power of a mom's love! If this is possible, then my long days with my children, are like a walk in the park. People always ask me how I balance it all: motherhood, my family, marriage, career and personal time. I tell them that it feels light to me. And when it doesn't, I seek support!

This brings me to the *stability of character*. Proverbs 31:25-27 says "Strength and dignity are her clothing, and she laughs at the time to come. She opens her mouth with wisdom, and the teaching of kindness is on her tongue. She looks well to the ways of her household and does not eat the bread of idleness." A mother's true character is loving, kind and wise. But how do we stay 'in character' when we're so busy, stretched to our limits and sometimes overwhelmed? Let's face it there are mothers that are not making the best choices for their children. Some are abusive whether it be emotionally or physically. Some mothers neglect their children, even choose to abandon them. And some mothers are simply making choices that cause their children some sort of hardship. *This indicates that something has happened to the mother, not that there is something wrong with the mother.* You see, we are all inherently worthy and when we become unaware of that very worthiness we get out of alignment with our true character. That's when we start showing up unloving, unkind and unwise.

There are many ways we lose sight of our worth but if I had to sum it up, it comes down to these three categories:

- *"Less Than" Messages:* We hear or learn something that makes us feel like we are not enough just as we are. We start to believe that we have to change something about ourselves in order to become worthy again.

- *Trauma:* We go through something deeply painful, shocking or overwhelming and as a result, we experience ourselves as broken. If we don't heal from the experience, then we remain in pain.

- *Our Circumstances:* We erroneously make our circumstances mean something about who we are in this world. Rather than identify with the truth about who we are - - that we are perfect, whole and complete and that doesn't change - - we identify with external measures of our worth.

So, if you find that you or a mother figure in your life, aren't being loving, wise, kind or nurturing, it may be time to pull away from the day to day and refuel your love tank.

Sometimes all it will take is a little self-care and other times, it will require deeper inner work. Don't be afraid to get support! Here are some options:

- Trusted loved ones
- Support groups
- Psychiatrists, Psychologists, therapists
- Life coaches
- Subject matter experts
- Classes, retreats, workshops
- Books, blogs, webinars

Whatever works for you, but don't continue to drift! Your babies, your family and the world needs you! Just like Lil' Mama needed me.

The next aspect of strength is *freedom of weakness*. Pertaining to mothers, I believe there is a recognition, consciously or unconsciously, that we aren't going to always get it right. We will have shortcomings, frailties, imperfections but they don't stop us from being who we need to be and doing what we need to do. We would be paralyzed if we stopped every time we thought we might fail. We probably couldn't get through a day! And yet, we keep going!

I remember when I was left with all three of my children for the first time. It was about four weeks after my son was born. Everyone who visited to help had traveled back to where they lived and my husband had gone back to work. It was just me and them. My two older girls were supposed to be getting ready for bath time but were, instead, running around half naked, screaming and dancing wildly. My son was crying waiting to be nursed. I didn't know which direction to turn and there was a moment when I was like "I can't do this!" I recall thinking, "what did I do?!" I was crying and in shambles but instead of folding, I called my friend who is a mother of four and at times a mentor to me. She gave it to me straight "You can do this, it's hard, but you can do this." It was just what I needed to hear. I pushed through that night and have moved forward ever since.

I know there are days I could have done better and on those days, I tell my babies "Tomorrow, I'll be more patient...I'll explain it more thoroughly...I'll take more time to listen...I will hug a little longer...I promise." They inevitably smile and say something like "Okay mommy" and it's as simple as that.

And here's another thing, if you are struggling with your relationship with your mother, have a lot of pain around your relationship with her, or you simply want more from her, please know, she did the best she knew to do. If she knew better, she would have done better and I invite you to let it go. Let her off the hook and let yourself off the hook so that you may experience your freedom. The same goes for your relationship with your father.

~ ON FORGIVING OUR PARENTS... ~

In my experience with helping people break through their internal barriers, I have found that many are working through issues with their parents. It doesn't matter at what age. This type of deep seeded pain will get in the way of the life of your dreams whether you are aware of it or not. So, if you fall into this category this is an opportunity for you to practice forgiveness. Forgiveness is the gateway to freedom from any destructive feelings you are harboring. It will liberate you, and in the context of your parents, it will lead you to a healthier understanding of them and appreciation for the role they play in your life.

Here are some steps you can take to forgive your mother, father or both:

1. Write a letter to your parent(s) explaining why you are hurting. Write, in detail, about all the experiences that have caused you pain. Don't edit yourself, simply let the words flow from your heart. Be willing to walk through the pain.

2. Read the letter out loud in front of a mirror or to someone you trust. This serves as your opportunity to feel heard.

3. On a new piece of paper, write "I forgive my [Insert mother or father] for..." Then proceed to complete this sentence for each painful event that you wish to release.

4. When you feel ready to forgive, sit down in front of a mirror and make eye contact with yourself. Without the list or anything else in your hands that might distract you, one by one, articulate your forgiveness statements. Don't worry about whether you remember what you wrote exactly. The power of this exercise is seeing what comes up for you organically.

5. After completing these steps, if there is an experience, insight or lesson you want to share with your parent(s) and it will support your healing, set up a meeting to speak with them. The intention is to further you along in the forgiveness process not to place blame or make them feel bad. It is your responsi-

bility to make sure that you are coming from a loving place.

If you are still hurt or angry, do not set up the meeting as it could backfire and turn into a negative experience. Equally important is ensuring you go into the conversation without any expectations. Your parents are not the ones on the healing journey, you are. Be clear about what you want to communicate and recognize they may not say what you want to hear. Let them express while you stay grounded in love. The goal is to share and foster a healthy conversation.

6. Be diligent about forgiveness and practice it on a regular basis. You want to clear out residual resentment, pain or any other negative feelings, that may be lingering about.

Finally, Mr. Filmore describes strength as the *power to withstand temptation.* I say this is the temptation to fold when it gets too rough. When we start to think we can't do it, it's too much, or we can't have it all, we've got the power to withstand buying into it! Mothers are presented with the challenge of raising their children while fulfilling any other dreams they may have. As a speaker and life coach, I have been so blessed to have the opportunity to build my career while raising my children. Yet, there have been times I've had to choose between them.

I once had a business appointment that I was committed to keeping because it could potentially lead to bringing my self-love work to a new demographic. A couple of days before the appointment, I realized that it conflicted with my son's Thanksgiving Feast performance. Now this was his first year of pre-school, so he didn't necessarily know that mommy was supposed to be there and I probably could have gotten away with a no-show. The problem was, I wouldn't be okay with a no-show. After all, he had been working really hard on memorizing his turkey songs, all over the house, for weeks and up to this point I had never missed any of my children's special performances. Authentically, I wanted to be in two places at one time so this was a tough choice. I prayed about it. I asked my friends what they would do if they were in my situation and I looked at every possible scenario for squeezing both appointments in. Ultimately, I ended up surrendering - - I released the emotional attachment to how the situation was going to turn out. Then, sure enough at 11 p.m. the night before, I received an email from the woman I was to meet with, asking if we could reschedule! The next day, my son sang his little heart out and he blew me the biggest kiss ever at the end of his performance.

The balancing act that mothers play is tremendous and it only works when we have a willingness to tend to ourselves as much as we focus our attention outward.

Remember, the love tank must be full at all times!

Chapter 7

What's a credit score got to do with me?

"Get your shopping on at the mall, max your credit cards
You don't have to choose, buy it all, so they like you
Do they like you?
Wait a second, why should you care what they think of you?
When you're all alone, by yourself, do you like you?
Do you like you?
You don't have to try so hard
You don't have to give it all away
You just have to get up, get up, get up, get up
You don't have to change a single thing"
- Try, A song by Colbie Caillat

MEAN

My credit score was 810. Banks were rolling out the red carpet for me. I was a young, single woman, making really good money and there wasn't a purchase I couldn't make, an account I couldn't open or a perk I wasn't offered. I even received courtesy calls thanking me for my business. I found it interesting that I was getting so much attention for simply being responsible with my financial commitments. So it was no surprise that I was granted a loan for an investment property when I called to ask for one.

I knew a lot of people who were "flipping" properties, or renting them out for a profit, and I was excited at the prospects of a new business venture. But it was an excitement that was quickly silenced by a major shift in the real estate market. Property values were dropping significantly each day. I started to feel hopeless because every time I checked the value of my investment home it was dropping further and further from the purchase price. I was constantly checking the financial news and hearing the horror stories of people losing their investments, going bankrupt or even becoming homeless. Fear was definitely in the air and I found myself sinking into it with each payment I made for the depreciating property.

One day, I made the decision to take the situation into my own hands. I set up an open house, advertised it, drove four hours to the property itself to find a renter! I was going to turn this situation around no matter what it took.

When I got to my condo, which up until that point, I had never physically seen, I realized what a gem it was. It was beautiful! All this time, I was so caught up in the monetary value of it, I did not appreciate what I really had. I felt better than ever about getting it rented. I laid my blanket out on the floor, put my headphones on and fell asleep.

My first call for an appointment came in at 9:05am! And that was the first of many. Everyone who came to see the apartment loved it. I even got a couple of offers to pay up to 6 months up front! This was better than I could have imagined. By the end of the weekend, I knew who I was going to go with. I chose to rent it to a young, newly employed, single mother looking to get out of an unhealthy relationship. She was not the most financially sound choice but she was the most sincere, committed and authentic one.

When I returned home and shared my good news with my friends, they immediately thought I was crazy for not choosing one of the potential renters that wanted to prepay months in advance. They wondered why I took the risk. All I could offer up at the time was "It just feels right."

And I was right! She was a loyal and easy renter for three years. When she was ready to move on to a new place, she called well in advance to let me know so that I would have a head start on finding a new renter. But when I got this call, my situation was completely different. I was recently married, had moved to another state, was expecting my first child and I was no longer in the same financial situation. I had just changed careers from steady paychecks in Corporate America to unpredictable income through entrepreneurship in the field of "making a difference." I was barely able to pay the difference between the rent she was paying and the actual amount of the mortgage each month.

When I left my well paying engineering job to do what I love, I had this grand plan of how I was going to roll out my new career. It was impressive. But God had other plans for me. Once I found out I was pregnant, I found myself frustrated with working and gravitating towards simply being, relaxing and enjoying this miraculous journey of pregnancy. I prayed and meditated to understand what was going on with me. Why wasn't I making progress with my goals? I realized that this time in my life was about becoming a mother rather than hitting the milestones that were so neatly laid out on my master plan.

Even though I was immersed in my pregnancy, there was still

part of me that was afraid to lose my financial credibility, my "red-carpet worthy" standing and the impact to my impeccable credit score. I immediately put the property back on the market and I took a temporary position making copies, filing and doing data entry, to try to pay the mortgage until it was sold.

I did temporary work until I was too pregnant to keep up. I poured every bit of money I made into the property but as soon as I stopped working I fell behind on the payments. I figured that I would focus on finishing my first book before the baby arrived and soon after I would go back to temping.

One day, I was finishing up hours of inspired writing when I received a discouraging email. I did not get a contract that I was depending on to make my next mortgage payment. I immediately got writer's block so I decided to head home. At nine months pregnant my belly barely fit behind the wheel. I decided to call the mortgage company to update them on when I would be able to make good on my next payment and immediately their tone was downright nasty. She was treating me as if I were a criminal Like I had gotten myself in this financial mess on purpose. She was interrogating me as if to prove I had done something wrong. I couldn't help but think they actually train their call agents, in this particular department, to be mean. It was just so foreign to me. After trying to answer her questions for several minutes, I finally exploded into tears, yelled into the phone "you can't treat people like this!" and hung up. At this point I had to pull my car over because even though I was using bluetooth, I felt like I was having an anxiety attack and driving was no longer safe. I was breathing heavy and out of control. My emotions were getting the best of me. I called my husband and he reminded me that the most important thing was the health of our baby. Eventually I calmed down.

I was only a couple months behind on my payments and gone

were the red carpets, nice treatment and "fabulous" offers. I was put in a category and I didn't know how to get myself out of it. I felt like a failure.

A few weeks later, I welcomed my first daughter into the world and the way I viewed everything changed! I wanted to do everything I could to make her life the best it could be and I wanted all of my choices to reflect that intention.

When the time came to decide whether I was going to go back to a job with a steady income, I was torn. I was torn between setting a good example of responsibility for my daughter and spending as much time as I could nurturing her and meeting her needs at such a young age.

I started temping again to get my finances back in shape. I was enjoying the company of my coworkers and I found the nature of the work fun but, after a few months, I was over it. I was miserable being away from my baby girl and even though the company offered me a permanent position, I resigned.

I went back to taking care of my baby full-time which reduced my availability for generating income significantly. Consequently, the property went into foreclosure which made me sad because I loved that little place. But I was done believing that the banks' lack of compassion and my downward spiraling credit score said anything about who I was on the inside. My priorities had changed and it was time for me to hold my chin up high and address the issue with dignity.

I had finally figured out that the most powerful lesson I could give my daughter was to show her I know I am worthy, even when other people, or my circumstances, might suggest otherwise.

TIME

This experience had me on a serious roller coaster even though at this point in my life, I was years into living from my *mean*. This is exactly how it happens. We get blindsided by an unexpected change in our finances and it triggers us to question our values. The positive effect is that it can also push us to hone in on what is most important to us and what really serves our highest good. As we learned in my case, these don't necessarily equate to being the most financially sound decisions.

I had to be reminded of this. Sometimes we're able to remind ourselves and sometimes it takes something external. My reminder in this case, came from a friend I hadn't seen in a while. Mark and I first met when my husband and I were starting a camp for teenagers that awakens them to the dreams in their hearts. I was telling everyone I knew about it, hoping to raise funds to help as many teenagers as we could. Even though we had just met, he put a check in my hands for a thousand dollar donation and said "If you're this passionate about the camp, I have to be a part of it." I was blown away by his belief in me. He didn't ask for proof, data or reports on where his money was going. This gave me powerful information about how I was showing up in the world. To this day I'm extremely grateful for that moment because it ignited a new confidence in myself and serves as a reminder whenever I'm having doubts.

It would be years after that moment, when Mark made another profound impact on my life. We were catching up one day when I mentioned that I had been temping to keep up with my bills.

This came as a shock to him because as far as he knew, I was busy changing the world. Within moments and without hesitation, he asked me why I was wasting my time and talents. He even asked how much per hour I was making, probably just so I could say it out loud and recognize the discrepancy between my pay rate and the value of my time. But the game changer for me was when he asked me "If you had to choose only three things to focus on, at this time in your life, what would they be?" The premise was that I couldn't focus on *anything* else. I immediately listed my family, the camps for teens and my mission of empowering women to love themselves. That was all I needed. Very soon after that talk, I quit temping.

ON COACHING…

Whether Mark knew it or not, he was coaching me. I have learned over the course of my coaching career that it only works when the "coachee" is ready. There was a time in my life that Mark's candor would have been unwelcomed but in this case, I was right where I was supposed to be, to receive the message loud and clear. Let me make a distinction here: Coaching is not simply someone advising you or giving you their opinion. *Coaching is supporting someone in gaining new insight about themselves that will forward them in the direction of their dreams.* We all have coaches placed carefully along our life journey. It's magical when their action meets our readiness.

 L O V E

Circumstances happen. We will experience financial fluctuations whether they are within our control or not. As long as we remain authentic through them, they will not define us. Somewhere along the way, we pick up the belief that our financial status actually means something about our worth. At that stage of my life, I was giving my credit score a whole lot of power. Power to sway my choices and manipulate my thoughts about myself. For a while there, I could not ditch the idea that I was giving up or that I was irresponsible. But the truth is, I am the person who rented to a struggling, young, single mother fleeing from domestic violence, simply because my heart led me to do so.

The question we get to ask is, *why do we give financial status so much power?*

The simple answer is because we are trained to. According to our society, money equals happiness. The rich are glorified and the poor are shunned. From our fascination with celebrities to workaholism to choosing high-paying careers that make us miserable, we have received the memo loud and clear: we *should* have lots of money.

But let's break it down further. According to Paula Gregorowicz, *"financial status is measured by our net worth, credit score, assets, liabilities, income, expenses, debt and insurance."* The problem here is that these are all quantitative measurements and the qualitative aspects, of a thriving financial status, are not taken into account. In this scenario, our feelings about ourselves will absolutely fluctuate with our finances because this definition is not founded on the unwavering truth that *we are born worthy of the best life has to offer!*

More times than not, we find it easier to go after making more money rather than doing the inner work it takes to break free from the misguided belief that more money means more worth. As a result, I offer up this definition to break that paradigm: *A thriving financial status means having purpose-driven income that affords you a life filled with your true desires - - people, experiences or things that you draw into your life because they are in alignment with your authentic self.*

In terms of career, there is an unrivaled level of fulfillment that comes with generating your income by living your purpose. Through all of my financial turmoil, never once did I regret leaving my engineering career and stepping into my purpose. It's hard to explain, because even though I had doubts about my financial choices, I woke up everyday with this passion in my heart that kept moving me in the direction of my dreams. Once you've got this kind of love for what you do, hold on tight and stay the course. That kind of love cannot fail.

If you want to be in discovery about your true financial status, cross-examine yourself with these questions:

If you want to be in discovery about your true financial status, cross-examine yourself with these questions:

❦ Why do you want money?

_____

_____

_____

❦ Do you currently have the things you want money for? Why or why not?

_____

_____

_____

How do you make your money?

❦ Are you passionate about what you do? If yes, why? If no, describe what you are passionate about?

_____

_____

❦ Does your passion serve a greater good? And how?

_____

_____

❦ Do you know without a doubt that your passion is your purpose? And how do you know?

_____

_____

Use your responses to these questions as a starting point to determine if you have a thriving financial status or whether you get to make some adjustments to achieve it.

You'll have some bumps along the way to achieving your thriving financial status but you'll also have some victories! In those victories, there are gems for us to learn and to celebrate! While I ended up giving up the rental property in the end, let's not miss the success in finding a renter during a recession. The distinction here is that we don't get to limit ourselves by facts, appearances or opinions. The facts were telling me that my property was depreciating and that there were twenty-nine other condominiums up for sale or rent just like it, in my complex alone! Realtors were telling me I'd never find a renter to pay what I was asking for and that I might as well give up. I could have easily thrown in the towel based on the "data" but I was not willing to do so. I knew in my heart, or authentically, that there was a way to make it happen. When I set my intention to get the condo rented and matched it with a commitment, like heading out there to get it done myself, I got results. If you're intention is based on a true desire, you will achieve your results. Just know that the results may not always come in the exact form you envisioned. But they will come and then it is time to celebrate!

To celebrate is to intentionally acknowledge and honor your success. This is a step that we tend to skip. We are more comfortable obsessing about what went wrong, what we did wrong or what is wrong with us. It's true, human beings tend to focus on the negative. In fact, it is scientifically proven that negative information is weighed more heavily than positive information. Researchers say it has to do with the evolutionary process when being aware of danger was critical to our survival. As such, our brains became conditioned to noticing negative stimuli. Perhaps this is why so many aspects of our society emphasize the negative and why it is so influential.

If you want to break free from this influence, it is on you to counter the negative messages you receive with a deliberate focus on the positive! *Consistently recognizing, appreciating and celebrating your successes instead of obsessing over your failures, is required.* This will take time because you may have a lot of reprogramming to do, so be patient with yourself and don't get discouraged. You are working on a paradigm shift that will result in a heightened awareness of the love, joy and goodness that runs through you, around you and for you.

Success - - the accomplishment of an aim or goal - - is relative. What you want to accomplish varies from anyone else in this world! What it requires of you to accomplish it, is unique to you as well. What may seem like a success to you, may not seem like a success to someone else but that does not make it any less significant. Every time we achieve a success, an attribute, or set of attributes, of ourselves is activated. There in lies the beauty. That is where you learn about your power to create love, joy and goodness in your life.

The following is an assignment that will help you establish a pattern of focusing on your successes and ultimately, create an extraordinary way of life:

Each day for *at least thirty days...*

- Write down a minimum of five successes - - things that went right.
- Reflect on why they are a success.
- Examine what it took for you to accomplish them.
- Record what you learned about yourself by using "I am..." statements. For example, I am perseverant. I am courageous. I am loving.
- Before the end of the day, honor yourself in a way that is meaningful for you.

Chapter 8

Our Bodies Need Love Too

"She has dreams to be an envy, so she's starving
You know, covergirls eat nothing
She says "beauty is pain and there's beauty in everything"
"What's a little bit of hunger?"
"I can go a little while longer," she fades away
She don't see her perfect, she don't understand she's worth it
Or that beauty goes deeper than the surface, oh, oh
So to all the girls that's hurting, let me be your mirror
Help you see a little bit clearer the light that shines within"

\- Scars to Your Beautiful, A song by Alessia Cara

MEAN

was at the point of exertion when my teeth were clenched and the veins in my neck were bulging out. This was not an uncommon condition during a challenging workout, but this time something did not feel right. Suddenly, in mid-pushup, a sharp pain shot through my shoulder and residual waves of pain continued. It felt as if something major ripped and smaller muscle fibers were tearing one by one. I was hell-bent on finishing my workout so I got in my zone - - a place in my mind that can ignore physical pain - - and pushed through. Once the adrenaline subsided, I was suddenly reacquainted with the pain and it hurt like hell.

I went home and iced my shoulder hoping that was the cure. I could feel the anxiety building up in me, not because of how serious the injury might be but because I did not want to miss even one day at the gym. Working out was more than just conditioning my body, it was my way of clearing my mind and feeding my soul.

I was afraid my primary doctor would tell me to stop working out altogether so I decided to go see my chiropractor who had helped me recover from previous ailments. He mentioned it could be an injury in my rotator cuff and that it could be serious. After treating me, he made some recommendations on how to let my shoulder heal. As most people respond to "recommendations," I carried out the ones I was willing to do. I iced it, took anti-inflammatories, taped it up for workouts and even continued my chiropractic appointments, but I did not let it rest.

Six weeks later, the pain was excruciating. I went back to my chiropractor who does not like to tell me what to do, but had to put it to me as straight as he could, "Anita, I almost want to put your arm in a sling to make sure you let it rest." I laughed and said "Now that would be serious!" Then he looked me in the eyes and said, "Anita, it is." It was in that moment that I finally got it. I had to take this seriously and let myself heal.

I ended up getting an MRI to ensure it wasn't more severe than we thought. I took three weeks off from my favorite gym classes and replaced them with running which did not aggravate the injury at all. I followed all of the recommendations he gave me. It was a slow recovery but two months later, my shoulder was back to normal.

TIME

Unfortunately, this was not the first time I got injured and didn't take proper care of myself. Rather, it was the first time it took so much time and attention to recover. I've been tackling tough workouts since I was sixteen years old and let's face it, back then it took two seconds to heal from whatever! It's been tough learning some of the changes our bodies go through as we get on in years. It happens right under our noses and while there are ways to reduce the effects of aging, we still get to acknowledge the changes. We need to honor the sense of loss for what our body once was so that we can make adjustments that serve the current version of our bodies. I've learned, the hard way, how important it is to exercise safely as well as adjust my hydration and nutritional intake, accordingly.

It's not just the changes in physical ability that can be discouraging but it's also the changes in physical appearance. Especially when we live in a society that places so much emphasis on looking younger. I've learned that whether we are ready or not, we get to love ourselves through all the changes so that we don't fall victim to the negativity spewed by society, or the people in our lives with these same views.

I used to work out because I was trying to fit societal norms. I was trying to make my body look like the ones I saw in magazines and on television. I also compared myself to the popular girls at school. So anything that seemed like an imperfection, I was going to try to melt it away through exercise. This was not authentic action, this was trying to be something I'm not for reasons that stemmed from feelings of inadequacy. While it compelled me to work out, I didn't enjoy it nearly as much as I do now.

Over the years, as I healed what was within, I honed into the real reasons being physically fit is important to me. I want to be the strongest, healthiest woman I can be for my family, for my community and for the world. I've got a lot of responsibilities and I get to be operating at my best.

L O V E

With all that said let's dive deeper into *fitness* and the role it plays in our overall health and our physical appearance. In simple terms, fitness is having good physical condition as a result of exercise and proper nutrition. More elaborately, it is the conditioning of our *"cardiorespiratory endurance (aerobic power), skeletal muscle endurance, skeletal muscle strength, skeletal muscle power, flexibility, balance, speed of movement, reaction time, and body composition"* (Office of Disease Prevention and Health Promotion, www.health.gov), through a regimen of exercise, diet and rest.

Fitness is a key component in having your *dream body* in terms of appearance and what your body is physically capable of achieving. We tend to focus on physical appearance because of societal influences, but think about it, our bodies are the vehicles through which we achieve our dreams. For example, I want to live to see my children get married. I want to be alive when they have children and I want to be an active part of my grandchildren's lives. My body plays a key role in my ability to achieve these dreams.

Now let me be clear, the *dream body* is relative. It is not cookie cutter. It is unique for every individual because we have distinct:

- 🌹 **Body types:** ectomorphs, mesomorphs, endomorphs, etc.

- 🌹 **Attributes:** age, gender, heredity, etc.

- 🌹 **Habits:** exercise, diet, self-talk, etc.

- 🌹 **Challenges:** sickness, disease, disability, etc.

- 🌹 **Purposes we serve:** runner, dancer, speaker, construction worker, engineer, gymnast, doctor, etc.

All combinations of these factors, must be loved and accepted as they are. Our bodies simply won't cooperate with us any other way! Our bodies are a barometer for what's happening on the inside. If you love your body, it will respond to your desires! If you do not love and appreciate your body, it will not show up or perform the way you want it to and it can even lead to health challenges.

I've come across so many women who criticize, shame, and who've given up on, their bodies. They don't find physical fitness to be achievable because they've tried every exercise and diet program under the sun. But those are just fragments of what it takes. What it really takes is putting authenticity into action!

Learn what it is you really want and be driven by your *true desires*. When you are in pursuit of that which you absolutely must have because it comes from deep down in your heart and soul, there is no stopping you. Remember, I want to play with my grandchildren. There is nothing I wouldn't do for that dream! Challenges will come our way. We'll get too busy. Our family will need us. We have other things to spend our money on. Your desires have the ability to override these barriers so make sure you're clear about what you want.

Let me also say that "failures" in physical fitness, simply mean you haven't found the perfect match for your body yet. So what! Let yourself off the hook. Release any shame, guilt or negative thoughts you have about it. Praise yourself for trying. Then move on to search for which physical activity brings you joy. Search for who will make it fun with you. Search for what challenges you in all the *right ways*. Play around until you find what works for *you*. You may have to get creative. You may need to step outside of your comfort zone. You will experience trial and error. It's simply part of the process.

In order for a muscle to grow, it *must* be pushed beyond it's current capability. At that point, the muscle actually breaks down and most of the time, this is when it will create an experience of soreness for us. Then the muscle mends itself, we feel better, and it becomes stronger. Everything in your life worth being, doing and having, calls for you to become the person it takes to make it happen. Achieving your dream body is no exception to the rule. As in building muscles, you will be required to push yourself beyond your norm. Then, you will probably experience some discomfort. You'll undergo a transformation and ultimately, you will produce results. You may as well enjoy the ride!

Chapter 9

All My Children

"I am changing, I'll get my life together now.
I am changing, yes, I know how.
I'm gonna start again.
I'm gonna leave my past behind.
I'll change my life.
I'll make a vow.
Nothings gonna stop me now"
- I Am Changing, A song by Jennifer Hudson

M E A N

My son was starting pre-school in a week. This was about to be my first dance with "empty nest" syndrome. All of my friends had been telling me it comes in phases but I didn't realize it would hit me like this. Soon, my time with my children would be reduced to evenings and weekends. While the thought of having so much free time to myself was enticing, there was a dark cloud hanging over my head that I could not shake. I couldn't stop thinking about what this really meant for me as a woman. My babies were growing up and the baby-making phase of my life was coming to an end. This was painful.

Technically, I could still get pregnant but I knew it would be too tasking on my body especially while giving my children the love and attention they deserve. And while it could be downright exhausting, I missed everything about the pregnancy phase. Never mind that I could barely walk for the last 6 weeks or that I passed a kidney stone, acquired three gall stones and fractured my pelvic bone as a result of my pregnancies. I suddenly had a deep yearning for the experience of growing a life inside of me again.

I missed the nursing phase even though I could clearly remember being frustrated with living my life in two to four hour intervals. I had always referred to nursing as a labor of love because, while it was difficult, even painful at times, the experience of feeding my babies and watching them grow simply from my milk, was exquisite. I kept thinking about their big beautiful eyes looking up at me as they suckled on my breast and then fell into a milk-induced slumber.

I even missed the sleepless nights and changing dirty diapers!

These were all tell tale signs that I could not shake this immense feeling of loss that was triggered by my youngest child starting pre-school.

A couple of days before Khaiden's first day, my husband came to me with an unprecedented request. A staff member at his church needed to take a leave of absence from a position that had proven challenging for anyone who stepped into it. Not necessarily because they weren't up for it but because it often led to burnout. He asked me if I would come into the position on an interim basis and do some consulting. He wanted me to clearly define the job description and eliminate any obstacles that were preventing it from being sustainable. If I accepted, I would be there for 30 days and it would be effective immediately.

I had to ask myself, why this opportunity was coming up for me? After all, wasn't I meant to finally have time to myself after the roller coaster of having three children in less than four years? And wasn't I meant to finally go all-in on my career to impact those millions of women I always talked about? I was confused because on the other hand, I loved my church and I wanted to help it succeed. I knew my background in operations would be a great asset.

After processing all of the pros and cons, I chose to accept the offer at the church. I just knew this would be the perfect distraction from the pain of dropping my baby off at pre-school. And it worked...eventually! The truth is, both my son and I were pretty upset with our new life. For two weeks or so, he orchestrated sit-ins on the floor of the pre-school lobby, silent protests, fits, forgetting-his-backpack sabotages and gave compelling arguments for why he should stay with mommy instead of going to school. While it made mornings a bit more challenging, I felt great knowing the feeling was mutual. We wanted to be together.

Eventually we embraced the change and it got easier. Whenever we did have some alone time, we cherished every moment.

TIME

I still get a pang in my heart every now and then, when I realize that I will no longer have another baby of my own. This is usually prompted by seeing an infant, a pregnant woman or even my children, who seem to have grown up in the blink of an eye. I believe that this is the case for any woman who has had children or who wanted children but did not have them. When our bodies can, or will, no longer produce another human being, we go through a grieving phase. And just because the loss of this significant part of ourselves is a natural progression of a woman, it doesn't necessarily make it any easier to process. Signs of grieving include feelings of sadness, yearning, crying, headaches, loss of appetite, difficulty sleeping, weakness, fatigue, aches, pains and other stress-related ailments.

It is more intuitive to grieve when we have experienced the loss of someone or something that we loved. For example, the loss of a loved one due to death or the end of a relationship, friendship or marriage. The loss of a job, and the paycheck that came with it, can be a blow. The loss of a home due to wildfires, hurricanes or earthquakes will hit us hard. But no matter what the source of the sorrow is, we must grieve until we arrive at a place of acceptance with the "new normal." You will know you are done grieving when you experience peace in your soul with the change.

Another thing I noticed during this phase of my life is that men handle these feelings much differently, even though they feel a sense of loss as well. Every now and then, after having three children together, my husband would say something like "Let's just have one more." Each time, I could see in his eyes that he meant it and that the idea just lit him up. Usually moments later, the reality of having a fourth child would hit and he would move on to a new topic. Yet every mention of having another child would take me on this inner emotional roller coaster that I would try to articulate, but he could never fully understand. While we have different experiences of this change in our lives, I really appreciate him sharing his feelings with me as it kept the lines of communication open to process and heal this part of us.

Working at the church added to the richness of my life. By saying yes to my husband's offer and to my baby boy growing up, I got to work with a team of people that quickly became my family. It brought me even closer to my husband and my spiritual community. It also broadened my experience in operations management and leadership. Overall, an amazing experience.

Even our most undesired life transitions require us to say a definitive "Yes!" to them. Not a tepid maybe or a begrudged, meager, angry yes, which is actually a "No!" By saying yes, we are clearing space, liberating our minds and opening our hearts to the change that is to come. We want to get to a place where we are ready to go all-in and play full out.

If we are experiencing any hesitation, we will find that fear, anxiety, worry, doubt or sadness for what once was, will play a role. Sometimes the influence is at the forefront of our minds and sometimes it plays softly in the background, making us resistant to the change.

Getting to a "Yes!" requires you to:

- *Be informed about the change to come.* This will help you navigate the change as well as help you remove as much fear of the unknown as possible.

- *Accept that it might be uncomfortable.* Navigating the part of the unknown that you can't whittle away with knowledge can feel uncomfortable. If you accept that there will be discomfort, then it tends to become smaller and not as influential.

❦ ***Know your options.*** You want to explore all of your options and be sure to think outside of the box to create options that energize you. You might even find a path that you're passionate about!

❦ ***Clear your heart.*** Find ways to quiet the emotions that do not serve you. Some common tools are:

1. Prayer
2. Meditation
3. Visualization
4. Breathing techniques
5. Emotional Freedom Technique/Tapping
6. Being in the silence
7. Listening to inspiring music
8. Talking to someone you trust
9. Exercising
10. Connecting with nature

This list is not all encompassing. It is simply meant to give you a few ideas. Everyone has their own unique ways of reconnecting to their inner strength, as you may have discovered in an exercise earlier on in this book. It's that inner strength that will overcome any unpleasant or negative emotions. And remember, if you get stuck, seek support.

❦ ***Accept the change.*** By this point you have recognized the authentic path to taking this change on, and it's time to welcome it. You want to formally say "Yes!" It is important to be very intentional about this step. It is your agreement with God, the Universe or your higher power, that you are open, ready and all-in!

❦ ***Have faith that all is well.*** You've done your homework and now it is time to enjoy your new experience. Stepping into the unknown is magical if we simply allow it to be. We learn more about who we are and what is possible in our lives.

Sure, it can be challenging to say yes to change, especially when we are emotionally attached to what was. But when we do the work to get to an authentic"Yes!", the rewards are undeniable.

Chapter 10

In the Name of Justice...

"Little black boys being killed in the streets
Bloody bodies, laying lifeless on the cold concrete...
They're being crucified by these homicides,
There's an ordinance against...all black lives...
Black women thrown in jail, and dehumanized
Can't post bail, commit suicide...
Pulled over for a simple traffic violation
Thrown and beaten on the ground, in humiliation."
- Black Lives Matter, A song by Rev. Charles Cooper Jr.

 M E A N

T he last time I felt like this, I had the "baby blues" which is the mildest form of postpartum depression. For one to two weeks after the birth of each of my children, I was weepy and cried at the drop of a dime over things I wouldn't normally cry over. This can be normal for women. In fact, approximately 80% of new mothers experience these "blues" due to body changes, hormone level fluctuation, exhaustion, anxiety, new routines and other factors. If I hadn't been reassured by my doctors and friends that this was normal and would go away in about two weeks, I would have thought I was depressed or at least what I had heard depression was like.

But this time, it wasn't the baby blues, it was yet another injustice that my heart just couldn't handle, causing me to be in and out of tears for days.

Two more black men had been killed at the hands of those who "serve to protect." I held it together when Trayvon Martin's shooter was exonerated. I got sick when cops shot Tamir Rice, a twelve year old boy sitting on a swing. I couldn't stomach when they choked the last breath out of Eric Garner. Then I went numb when an officer shot Mike Brown a twelfth time as his hands were up in the air. But the videos of the Alton Sterling and Philando Castile shootings made me want to explode! Not only were they killed using what is so obviously excessive force, but the cops were placed on paid administrative leave. They got to live. They got to be comfortable and they were free. I didn't believe for one moment that justice would be served and I knew with everything in me, that they weren't going to get anything worse than a slap on the hand. That level of hopelessness was daunting.

I could not go another moment without mourning. I was sorrowful for all of the victims, their families, my family, black people and the world. The tears were flowing and I was slumped over, head down with my face engulfed by my trembling hands, wondering "what the hell??!!!" I was beginning to wonder where God was in all of this. I hadn't felt this level of despair in a really long time.

My three-year-old Afro-Latino son was sleeping peacefully down the hall, cuddled in his big-boy bed, adorned with sheets that have little yellow characters known as Minions, seemingly watching over him while he slept. As beautiful as that sight was, I didn't feel safe anymore. Any one of these murdered black men, could be my son one day. My mind was involuntarily running through horrifying scenarios of what could happen to my son. I was angry, sad and scared all at once and each emotion seemed to be vying for my surrender. I wanted to scream at the top of my lungs and any minute I was going to punch the walls.

Everywhere I turned, my despair was corroborated. With each flip of a channel, there was no mention of these cases yet social media was going wild with news that these murderers were being exonerated. A statement was being made loud and clear to me, "black lives didn't matter." My children's lives didn't matter.

Water cooler chats ended there. They consisted of emotionally charged words, with no action behind them. There was also a collective "waiting for superman" attitude, where we just knew leaders were going to step up and handle the problem. But the reality was that even the President of the United States of America, an African American man, couldn't stop the snowball effect of what was happening.

"Where do I even begin?" I honestly thought I was doing my part to help transform our world into one where everyone is loved and valued, but I hadn't made a dent. The magnitude of what needs to be done, to arrive at a place where black men are no longer being shot down because of the color of their skin, was overwhelming.

I was ready to throw in the towel. My mind was clouded and my heart was broken and I couldn't see my way out of the haze.

TIME

Many years prior to this experience, I had done the inner work to heal my own identity issues regarding race.

I grew up in Brooklyn, New York where, on any given day, I was surrounded by every race, ethnicity and culture you could imagine. It was a fantastic way to see and experience the world. We are all one and we can all get along...for the most part.

It wasn't until I experienced racism and prejudice, that I got a taste of being treated 'less than' because of the color of my skin and my ethnicity. For some reason, I was always either too Puerto Rican or not Puerto Rican enough. I heard it all. My hair is too big and puffy. My skin is too dark. I've been called Mamacita, MariaConchita, Cuchifrito, wetback. I've been told that all I eat is rice and beans. I've been teased and taunted. I've been spat on. I've had women clutch their purses when I passed by. I've been whispered about and I've been ostracized.

On the flip side, I didn't speak Spanish enough. My last name didn't sound Latino. My skin was too white. My parents are too American. As if any of this changed the fact that I was actually Puerto Rican! But sure enough, I was young and impressionable so I let it all get into my head. I was confused about who I was and believed that I was not enough. As a result, I spent many of my childhood years trying to fit in.

It wasn't until I realized I was never meant to *fit in*, that I fell in love with my skin color which happens to change seasonally. I embraced my big hair that everyone loves to touch, and ask questions about, out of their own curiosity. I became proud of the Spanish that I am able to speak. I appreciated, even more, the Puerto Rican recipes my mother had passed down to me. The journey to arrive at this awareness was painful and I vowed never to hurt anyone because of the color of their skin or their ethnicity, in the ways I had experienced. As such, I was hesitant to even engage in any conversations that might trigger that kind of pain again.

But the shootings of these young black men woke me up. I could no longer ignore the conversation of race in our country and act like racism and biases do not exist.

It was time to face the music because it was more painful to turn a blind eye.

 L O V E

We can be triggered in the blink of an eye when love doesn't prevail. We can slip in consciousness and forget everything that we know and believe about who we are and what we can accomplish. And the longer we stay in the erroneous belief that anything other than love can win, the longer we stay disempowered. Transforming the world to one that only harbors love, in its many forms, requires each of us to do our part. Sometimes the task at hand, like ending something as hateful as racism, can seem insurmountable. Like our efforts won't change anything. This can cause us to believe it's not worth trying and if you couple that with all the diminishing messages we get from outside sources that tell us we can't, we may just forget how powerful we truly are. Margaret

Mead says *"Never doubt that a small group of thoughtful, committed citizens can change the world; indeed, it's the only thing that ever has."* I would add to the end of that *"and it starts with you!"*

I understand it can be challenging to remind ourselves of the truth about ourselves, when life continues to unfold at full throttle. The truth is, we are powerful beyond measure, when we are clear about who we are and we align our actions accordingly. You see, our morals, values, spirituality, dignity and integrity are, in fact, our roadmaps out of hopelessness and despair. Whether it is our…

- ❧ Knowledge that provides us with understanding
- ❧ Faith that gives us belief when there is no evidence
- ❧ Innate state of worthiness that activates our confidence
- ❧ Passion that presses us into action, or
- ❧ Commitment to playing a role in transforming this world

All of it will catapult us out of disbelief in ourselves and into a willingness to rise above the influence of our emotions to create something unprecedented in our lives and, consequently, in the world.

Soon after these days of despair, there was spark in me. I could no longer stay silent. The first thing I did was address the Sacramento County Board of Supervisors to voice my concerns about racially charged police brutality and murders. I started speaking out at my events, at my church, at the gym, on social media, in dinner conversation and with who ever was willing to have these tough talks so that we can find solutions. I was all in.

My son gets to know his worth.
My son gets to be proud of who he is.
My son gets to live.

Chapter 11

Not my President...

"When the silence isn't quiet
And it feels like it's getting hard to breathe
And I know you feel like dying
But I promise we'll take the world to its feet
And move mountains
We'll take it to its feet
And move mountains
And I'll rise up
I'll rise like the day
I'll rise up
I'll rise unafraid"
- Rise Up, A song by Andra Day

MEAN

was sitting on the couch with my daughters watching election results roll in. This was not an ordinary day. We were sitting in anticipation of watching the first woman, in United States history, be elected to the presidency. It was a surreal moment and I was ready to celebrate. My husband had invited a few friends over that evening and even put some hors d'oeuvres out in honor of the occasion.

Admittedly this woman, who was the first to win a major party primary, was not exactly America's favorite politician but I was personally proud of her ability to poke holes in the impenetrable "glass ceiling" over the course of her career and arrive at this accomplishment. I was all for our country taking another meaningful step towards equality and I was excited for my daughters to witness it. The only President they knew was, in fact, a black man. Now they were about to see a woman become president, as if all of this were the norm here in the United States.

The opposing candidate was a rich business man with no experience in government. He was also known for white supremacist views, misogynistic ways and being a loose cannon. The idea of him becoming president was scary on so many levels but, lucky for me, I didn't think he had a chance. I had been following various prediction models up to this point, and they were all showing he was going to lose.

Boy was I wrong and so were the experts! I watched in horror as the "racist misogynist," as I often referred to this candidate, was being declared the winner state by state. I immediately felt sick. Actually, it felt like someone punched me in the gut. I ran upstairs to my closet, away from my children and our company. I had to scream. I had to cry. I had to call my daddy.

My father was still holding out hope because there were a few results that hadn't come in yet. He was trying so hard to comfort me and calm me down as he normally would when things didn't go my way politically. But this time it was different. The idea that this many people in the country I lived in, voted for him, was an absolute blow. I was hurting. As a woman of color, a sexual assault survivor, the mother of three black children and someone who had humble beginnings, this blatant approval of racism, white supremacy, misogyny, bigotry and elitism on the "big screen" was personal. Personal in a way that went way deeper than my candidate not winning or party politics. This felt like I was being assaulted all over again and the idea that it would go on for at least four years, was even more invasive.

I was crying so loud that my children ended up finding me in the closet. I could see the concern on their faces as they simultaneously jumped in my arms and frantically asked what was wrong. As I explained to them that I was sad about our country, my eldest says *"Did the bad man win?"* - - as she and her classmates had coined him. I said yes, he did.

The next day, I did not want to get out of bed but I had to and it was like waking up before a nightmare was over. I walked through my morning ritual dazed, incomplete and traumatized yet I still managed to get my babies ready for school. As we drove to their school, a large black pick up truck with a huge confederate flag hoisted out of the back, screeched by us. My five year old son did not skip a beat and quickly asked "Mommy what does that flag mean?" I held back my tears, and fury, to mutter, "I'll tell you later son."

Racism was not new to me and, certainly, not new to our country, but racists emboldened by their "win" were flat out sickening. This feeling sucked and I was ready to talk about it. I posted something on social media that alarmed a few of my friends and the calls started coming in. I spoke with my mentor. I spoke with my bestie. I spoke with cousins and had several more rounds with my sister, mother and father. All attempts to make sense of how I'm feeling and trying to forge a path forward.

One particular call stood out for me. My friend Melissa had

asked me "Why don't you hold a rally at the state capitol?" I had shut the idea down pretty quickly as I didn't know anything about that kind of stuff and it made me a little uncomfortable -- in a knee-shaking kind of way. It just seemed too big for little 'ole' me especially when I felt so downtrodden.

My rationale for being a 'no,' was that I was already plugging away at the ills of the world through my life's work of empowering women to love themselves. I was confident that needed to remain my focus.

But for some reason, her question was haunting me well into the night and suddenly, I said to myself "Yes! Who am I not to have a rally?!" Something just clicked.

Within forty-eight hours, I had a concept, a date selected, a permit for the state capitol, my rally speakers lined up, a public relations expert, a graphic designer and a small group of people ready to help with anything. We called it "Women Stand Up for Equality!" Things were rolling and being busy was helping me cope. I was learning so many new things about myself, my capabilities and people. Between all of that, tending to my children and my career, I was filled to the brim. I had no time to wallow in my feelings.

With each day, things were unfolding in greater and more unimaginable ways, with such ease and grace. Out of the blue, my dear friend, Ester Nicholson, called to let me know that she had a gig in Southern California and that she was going to rearrange her flights so that she can make it to Sacramento just in time for the rally! She explained that she couldn't miss this moment in my life. I was blown away. We had become fast friends prior to this point. It was one of those experiences where we both agreed that we were probably best friends, or even sisters, in a previous lifetime. But she was also a well-known author, speaker and singer/songwriter doing powerful work in the world and I could not believe she was coming for me! I was deeply humbled and our friendship had just grown tenfold.

Now, Ester wasn't coming to sing but I just felt like I had to ask! A couple days later I called my friend and asked her if she would sing her song *"I Believe this Belongs To You"* at the rally. The song is about an incident when Martin Luther King, Jr. was spit in the face by a racist and his response was to take out his handkerchief, wipe the spit from his face and give it back to the man letting him know "I believe this belongs to you." When she said yes, I was overwhelmed with gratitude. The lineup was really coming together and I could feel an amazing experience coming on.

The night before the rally, a few of us were laughing and chatting as we created demonstration signs. Our perfectly heartfelt messages, imperfectly made their way onto poster board. Artists we were not but we were in great spirits! I didn't let on but I could feel something big brewing in me. A sensation was traveling through my body letting me know that something monumental was on it's way. The feeling was familiar. I felt this way before I made the jump from engineering to entrepreneurship.

"Women Stand Up for Equality" was a success! There were tears, cheers and emotions flying. We bonded together and people were inspired! We achieved a boost for the journey ahead as we entered into this twisted era of United States history.

At the end of the rally I announced that I was starting an organization called *Women For Equality* and asked people to sign up if they were interested. We got an overwhelming response and that's how the Sacramento-based grassroots organization that rises up in the name of love and equality, began.

TIME

Well, we've heard it a thousand times *"When life gives you lemons, make lemonade."* Women For Equality is my lemonade! I am so proud of the organization for bringing awareness to issues that are critical for creating a world that works for all and for giving people the opportunity to be heard and take action accordingly.

The resilience it took for me to turn my pain and fear into something so positive, has had profound staying power. I can no longer go into hiding. I've been found out. This is a great feeling and, at times, unsettling. You see, when you learn what you are truly capable of, as I did, you never know what the next big thing is and how much it will make your knees shake. And even though it's uncomfortable and stretchy, you know you will rise to the occasion. It's like always having what Dr. Carol Dweck calls a *growth mindset "which is the understanding that abilities and intelligence can be developed."* Rather than believe you're working with limited knowledge and ability, you know you will become the person it takes to achieve the audacious goal at hand.

Another result of stepping into leadership in this new way was an expanded understanding of equality. I had already been speaking out against racism and police brutality but once I was on this broader platform, my perspective on equality, had to transcend my own personal experiences, beliefs and thoughts. I had to expand past what I could see through my Puerto Rican female cisgender eyes.

It meant going into new spaces to listen and learn. Not making my opinions mean more than anyone else's. Not taking it personal when I didn't relate or felt left out. Feeling left out is a trigger for me. It makes me feel sad, unsafe and unloved. Sometimes I can shift immediately and sometimes I need time to process my feelings.

When I cross-examined why this happens, I learned that it stems from my childhood. I did not grow up around a lot of Puerto Ricans, other than my family. I grew up around mostly West Indians - - Jamaicans, Haitians and Trinidadians, to be more specific. For the most part, I was embraced in the community with open arms and I enjoyed it. To this day, I love Dancehall (a genre of Jamaican popular music) and I eat lots of Jamaican food. I understand Patois and enjoy many other aspects of the culture. Unfortunately, as I touched on earlier, there were times when people questioned my "Puerto Rican-ness" or reminded me that I am not West Indian and it made me think I didn't have a "village" - - a community that fully supported me. I now *know* this is not the case but every now and then when I feel excluded, I go right back to those erroneous thoughts. Luckily, I know how to get right back to my truth.

It is also worth mentioning that this is an example of how our values - - *those qualities that you find desirable or have an emotional investment in* - - start playing out in our lives. Because of my experiences with being included and excluded in different cultural circles, I am clear that its my true desire for all people to feel included. As such, I am passionate about inclusion and it is rooted in my life's work.

In my quest for inclusion and equality, I get to be conscious of what I am bringing into a space. This is not about me. This is far greater. We're talking about a *world* that works for everyone.

LOVE

My question to you is: *What are you a stand for?*

Being a stand is distinct from taking a stand for yourself, some-one else or some thing. To be a stand is the embodiment of your values, morals, spirituality, integrity and dignity. You bring it with you wherever you go. People see, feel, hear and experi-ence it. For example, I am self-love. It is integral to all aspects of who I am. I can't separate it from who I am, how I show up and my actions. If I'm speaking with a woman at the gym and she says "I'm fat." I immediately recognize she is not being kind to herself and I will say something kind. Please note, I will not tell her 'shouldn't' say that as that is unkind! But I can't help it, I demonstrate, create and support self-love.

To *take a stand* means to advocate for, or to represent, ourselves, someone else or some thing. Through my words of kindness, I took a stand for the woman at the gym, whether she was aware of it or not. And that's how it works! You are a stand because of who you are, and who you are, leads you to take a stand.

I took a stand by founding Women For Equality. My choice to do so, stemmed from my desire to support women, myself included, in expressing themselves - - a key step in the process of self-love - - and giving them a platform for their voices to be heard.

When its time to take a stand, you will get a prompting in the form of a strong feeling, a sign or dissonance. It will be up to you to discern when, and how, you follow through on the prompting.

I was prompted to expand the work I do with women by the intense feelings I had after the election but my choice to follow through came because I was ready to go to my next level. All areas of my life were aligned for this moment. Let me give you some examples of how things were lined up to support my decision. In Family, my children were now at an age where they could understand, and adjust to, mommy's absence from the home on a more frequent basis. In Career, I had just let go of a part time job that freed up some time. In Community, I was already speaking out on key issues. In Spirituality, I felt like I was being called forth to be more.

None of which meant I knew what I was doing! Going to your next level means that you are choosing to improve or develop an area of your life because it is aligned with your authentic self. Sometimes "the how" comes later and at times you will need to just trust the process. The good news is that when you choose to go to your next level authentically, it is driven by love and love perseveres.

Had I stayed sad and angry after the election, those emotions would not have gotten me far. When I processed those feelings and could think clearly again, I found my love-driven idea.

At the end of the day, that is what it is all about: love. Love is everything.

∼◦⟊◦⟊ IN CLOSING... ⟊◦⟊◦∼

Remember, the *life of your dreams is a string of extraordinary moments produced by you, and for you, that results from the process of self-love.* Living the life of your dreams is your birthright. You are meant to be, do and have all the goodness that life has to offer. When you lose sight of this truth and get triggered beyond your *mean*, be willing to do the work it takes to find your way back. You are worth the work of self-love. It may not always be easy but the reward is extraordinary living and the context of your life will always be love, in the many ways it shows up.

It is from this place that you will awaken to your love-driven ideas that will make this world the best world it can be. A world where *all* people have the freedom to unwaveringly know, love and express their authentic selves. Imagine if every person in this world is living an extraordinary life. There'd be no more hate, no more suffering, no more injustice, no more violence. Oh what a world this could be!

It's the vision I hold in my heart and I thank you for the role you play in it.

I truly believe it's up to women. We can make it happen. We are that powerful!

With that, I will sign off by simply letting you know that I love you. Because I do, just as you are.

ABOUT THE AUTHOR

Anita Ross is on a mission to empower millions of women to love themselves fully and to equip them with the tools for making choices that serve their highest good. Anita's life path has taken her through unique experiences that have allowed her to discover her purpose early in life. She knows firsthand the struggles that women face with low self-esteem, gender discrimination, body image pressures and domestic violence.

She teaches women the breakthrough principles and practices that she used to rescue herself from the quicksand of low self esteem and victim mentality to skyrocket herself to the mountaintop of total self acceptance and unconditional love. Her background as an engineer in Corporate America, an entrepreneur, the founder of a not-for-profit organization and a Life Coach all add to the rich experience she brings to her workshops, retreats and clients.

Since 2006, Anita has been serving women from all walks of life including, but not limited to, those of Women Escaping a Violent Environment (WEAVE, Inc.), My Sister's House, La Casa De Las Madres, Stockton County Foster Education Program, San Mateo Human Services Agency, San Joaquin Delta College, Solano College Umoja Program Scholars, Consumes River College, Delta Sigma Theta, Inc., Susan G. Komen and 51%, the women's group at the renowned advertising agency Wieden + Kennedy. She is the author of two self-help books for women, *"Mean Time Love: A Woman's Journey From Self-Loathe to Self-Love"* and *"Mean Time Love: So I've Got Self-Love, Now What?"* She is currently touring the country with her Mean

Time Love talks, workshops and retreats.

In 2016, Anita founded the grassroots organization, Women For Equality, that informs, inspires and empowers people to stand up for love and equality. She leads this growing organization in mobilizing through rallies, marches, protests, phone banking, events, joining forces or whatever is necessary, to ultimately achieve a world that works for everyone. Through her work with Women For Equality she leads a leadership team comprised of dedicated volunteers and together they have organized key events such as the Women Stand Up For Equality rally, the Women Stand Up For the Soul of America rally and the Racial Healing in America conference.

Anita earned a Bachelor of Science in Engineering degree from Stony Brook University in New York. She also holds a Master of Science in Engineering from the University of Michigan at Dearborn. Her professional work also includes holding key leadership, project management, strategic planning, operations, design, analytical and advisory positions over her ten year career for various Fortune 500 companies in Corporate America.

From 2002 to 2006, Anita embarked upon her entrepreneurial career and co-founded a consulting firm called StockTheMind, LLC. The firm serviced small and mid-sized businesses, supporting them with creating systems for growth and efficiency. It was during this time that she decided to merge all of her unique business skills with her passion for empowering women and teen girls.

Anita is married to author, radio personality, inspirational speaker and ordained minister, Kevin Kitrell Ross. Together they reside in Sacramento, California with their two daughters and a son.

Are you a woman in a relationship
that you know isn't working for you?

Are you a woman struggling to have
your voice heard?

Are you a woman who spends more time
taking care of others than yourself?

Are you a woman who spends more money
on clothes than you can afford?

Are you a woman who eats too much
or who does not eat enough?

Are you a woman who is too busy
to spend a moment alone?

If you answered yes to one or more of these questions,
you want to attend the next

MEAN TIME LOVE RETREAT

This transformational retreat is designed specifically for women to discover who they are, fall in love with who they are and be who they are...like no kidding! Together we will learn, laugh, explore, discover, heal, forgive and maybe even shed a tear or two, all in a safe, loving environment designed for you to go to your next level!

You will get to *know, love* and *express* yourself like never before. Come discover how loving your authentic self leads you to the life of your dreams no matter what you've been through, what other people think of you or what circumstances stand in your way!

You will leave with new awareness, distinctions and tools for achieving unconditional love and total self-acceptance.

For retreat schedule or booking information, please visit us at: www.anitaross.net

Like us on Facebook at: www.facebook.com/meantimelove

Do you find yourself veering off
your authentic path when adversity strikes?

Are losses, breakups or abandonment
major triggers for you?

Does it take you a long time to
get back to you once you've been triggered?

Do body changes or aging make you cringe?

Are you struggling with making
enough time for yourself?

Has a medical condition or health challenge
gotten you down?

Do you want to get your fears in check
once and for all?

If you answered yes to one or more of these questions, you want to attend the next

"SO I'VE GOT SELF-LOVE, NOW WHAT?" RETREAT

This powerful experiential retreat will support you in navigating life from a place of unconditional self-love and total self-acceptance like no kidding! Let's face it, life happens and even when we're ate the height of self-love we have our off days! Those moments in time when we doubt ourselves, regret our choices, forget our worthiness or lose sight of our vision.

You will leave with transformative experiences, powerful tools and key distinctions for persevering through life's challenges authentically and prevailing right into the life of your dreams!

For retreat schedule or booking information,
please visit: www.anitaross.net

Like us on Facebook at: www.facebook.com/meantimelove